Sales Metrics and Analytics

Tracking Performance for Growth

Kiet Huynh

Table of Contents

CHAPTER I Introduction 5
  1.1 Purpose of Sales Metrics and Analytics 5
    1.1.1 Understanding the Importance of Performance Tracking 5
    1.1.2 Goals of Sales Metrics Implementation 7
  1.2 Importance of Tracking Performance for Growth 11
    1.2.1 Impact on Revenue Generation 11
    1.2.2 Enhancing Operational Efficiency 13

CHAPTER II Understanding Sales Metrics 17
  2.1 Definition and Types of Sales Metrics 17
    2.1.1 Leading vs. Lagging Indicators 17
    2.1.2 Revenue Metrics 20
    2.1.3 Activity Metrics 22
  2.2 Key Performance Indicators (KPIs) in Sales 27
    2.2.1 Customer Acquisition Cost (CAC) 27
    2.2.2 Customer Lifetime Value (CLV) 30
    2.2.3 Sales Conversion Rate 34
  2.3 Setting SMART Goals for Sales Metrics 38
    2.3.1 Specific 38
    2.3.2 Measurable 41
    2.3.3 Achievable 44
    2.3.4 Relevant 47
    2.3.5 Time-bound 49

CHAPTER III Implementing Sales Analytics 58
  3.1 Data Collection and Management 58
    3.1.1 Identifying Relevant Data Sources 58

TABLE OF CONTENTS

    3.1.2 Data Quality Assurance 61

    3.1.3 Data Integration 63

3.2 Tools and Technologies for Sales Analytics 67

    3.2.1 CRM Systems 67

    3.2.2 Business Intelligence (BI) Tools 70

    3.2.3 Predictive Analytics Platforms 73

3.3 Data Visualization Techniques 77

    3.3.1 Dashboard Design Principles 77

    3.3.2 Visualization Best Practices 79

    3.3.3 Interpretation of Visual Data 82

CHAPTER IV Sales Forecasting Techniques 86

4.1 Historical Data Analysis 86

    4.1.1 Time Series Analysis 86

    4.1.2 Trend Analysis 91

    4.1.3 Seasonality Considerations 97

4.2 Predictive Modeling 106

    4.2.1 Regression Analysis 106

    4.2.2 Machine Learning Algorithms 113

    4.2.3 Forecast Accuracy Metrics 120

4.3 Market Trends Analysis 128

    4.3.1 Competitor Analysis 128

    4.3.2 Industry Research 133

    4.3.3 Economic Indicators 141

CHAPTER V Performance Evaluation and Optimization 149

5.1 Assessing Sales Team Performance 149

    5.1.1 Individual Performance Metrics 149

    5.1.2 Team Performance Metrics 152

    5.1.3 Performance Reviews and Feedback 155

TABLE OF CONTENTS

5.2 Identifying Areas for Improvement 161
    5.2.1 Gap Analysis 161
    5.2.2 Root Cause Analysis 167
    5.2.3 SWOT Analysis 173

5.3 Strategies for Optimization 177
    5.3.1 Training and Development Programs 177
    5.3.2 Process Improvement Initiatives 180
    5.3.3 Incentive Structures 184

CHAPTER VI Leveraging Analytics for Strategic Decision Making 189

6.1 Utilizing Sales Data for Strategic Planning 189
    6.1.1 Market Segmentation Strategies 189
    6.1.2 Product and Pricing Strategies 193
    6.1.3 Expansion and Diversification Opportunities 195

6.2 Adapting to Market Changes 199
    6.2.1 Agility in Decision Making 199
    6.2.2 Scenario Planning 204
    6.2.3 Risk Management Strategies 209

6.3 Incorporating Feedback Loops 214
    6.3.1 Continuous Improvement Processes 214
    6.3.2 Customer Feedback Integration 219
    6.3.3 Employee Engagement and Feedback Mechanisms 225

Appendices 232
    Useful Software and Platforms 232
    Conclusion 236

CHAPTER I
Introduction

1.1 Purpose of Sales Metrics and Analytics

1.1.1 Understanding the Importance of Performance Tracking

Sales metrics and analytics play a pivotal role in modern business strategies, offering invaluable insights into the performance of sales teams, individual representatives, and overall organizational effectiveness. In this section, we delve into the purpose of sales metrics and analytics, with a specific focus on understanding the importance of performance tracking.

Understanding the Importance of Performance Tracking

Performance tracking within sales operations is not merely a recommended practice; it is a fundamental aspect of achieving sustainable growth and success in today's competitive landscape. By comprehensively understanding the significance of performance tracking, organizations can leverage data-driven insights to optimize their sales processes, enhance efficiency, and drive revenue growth.

Informing Strategic Decision-Making: Performance tracking empowers organizations to make informed strategic decisions by providing real-time visibility into sales activities, trends, and outcomes. By analyzing key metrics such as conversion rates, customer acquisition costs, and sales pipeline velocity, decision-makers gain valuable insights that inform resource allocation, product development, and market expansion strategies.

Identifying Strengths and Weaknesses: Effective performance tracking enables organizations to identify both strengths and weaknesses within their sales operations. By evaluating individual and team performance metrics, managers can pinpoint areas of excellence and areas requiring improvement. Whether it's refining sales techniques, addressing skill gaps, or optimizing sales territories, performance tracking serves as a diagnostic tool for enhancing overall sales effectiveness.

Facilitating Continuous Improvement: Continuous improvement lies at the heart of successful sales organizations. Performance tracking facilitates this process by fostering a culture of accountability, transparency, and goal-oriented behavior. By setting clear performance benchmarks and regularly monitoring progress against these metrics, sales teams are motivated to strive for excellence and continuously raise the bar for success.

Enhancing Sales Coaching and Training: Performance tracking serves as a foundation for targeted sales coaching and training initiatives. By analyzing performance data at both individual and team levels, sales managers can tailor coaching programs to address specific skill gaps, reinforce best practices, and provide actionable feedback for improvement. Furthermore, performance data can be used to identify high-performing individuals who can serve as mentors or role models within the organization.

Optimizing Resource Allocation: Resource allocation is a critical aspect of sales management, and performance tracking plays a pivotal role in optimizing resource allocation decisions. By analyzing performance metrics alongside factors such as market demand, customer demographics, and product lifecycle stages, organizations can allocate resources—whether it be personnel, marketing budgets, or technological investments—in a manner that maximizes ROI and supports sustainable growth objectives.

Driving Accountability and Results: Performance tracking fosters a culture of accountability within sales organizations, where individuals take ownership of their targets and results. By establishing clear performance metrics and KPIs, organizations create a framework for accountability, where individuals are held accountable for their contributions towards overarching business goals. This accountability mindset not only drives individual performance but also cultivates a sense of collective responsibility towards achieving organizational success.

Adapting to Market Dynamics: In today's dynamic business environment, adaptability is key to survival and success. Performance tracking equips organizations with the agility to adapt to changing market dynamics, customer preferences, and competitive pressures. By monitoring leading indicators and predictive metrics, organizations can proactively identify emerging trends, seize new opportunities, and mitigate potential risks before they escalate into significant challenges.

Fostering Data-Driven Culture: Performance tracking cultivates a data-driven culture within sales organizations, where decisions are based on empirical evidence rather than intuition or anecdotal observations. By leveraging data analytics tools and technologies, organizations can harness the power of big data to extract actionable insights, identify patterns, and forecast future performance trends. This data-driven approach not only enhances decision-making accuracy but also instills confidence in the efficacy of strategic initiatives.

In essence, the importance of performance tracking within sales operations cannot be overstated. From informing strategic decision-making to driving accountability and fostering a culture of continuous improvement, performance tracking serves as a cornerstone of organizational success in today's hyper-competitive marketplace. By embracing data-driven methodologies and leveraging advanced analytics tools, organizations can unlock new avenues for growth, innovation, and sustainable competitive advantage.

1.1.2 Goals of Sales Metrics Implementation

Implementing sales metrics and analytics serves various strategic objectives aimed at enhancing organizational performance, driving revenue growth, and maximizing profitability. In this section, we explore the key goals associated with the implementation of sales metrics, highlighting their significance in optimizing sales operations and achieving sustainable business success.

Performance Evaluation and Benchmarking:

One of the primary goals of sales metrics implementation is to enable organizations to systematically evaluate the performance of their sales teams, processes, and strategies. By establishing key performance indicators (KPIs) aligned with overarching business objectives, organizations can measure performance against predetermined benchmarks and industry standards. This allows for the identification of areas of strength and weakness, enabling targeted interventions to improve performance where necessary. Additionally, performance benchmarking facilitates comparative analysis against competitors and peers, providing valuable insights into relative market positioning and performance gaps.

Goal Setting and Alignment:

Sales metrics implementation facilitates the setting of clear, measurable goals that align with broader organizational objectives. By defining specific, achievable targets for sales teams and individuals, organizations provide clarity of purpose and direction, fostering a sense of accountability and motivation among sales personnel. Moreover, aligning sales goals with broader business goals ensures coherence and synergy across functional areas, facilitating coordinated efforts towards common objectives. This goal alignment enhances organizational agility and responsiveness, enabling adaptive strategies in response to evolving market conditions and business priorities.

Forecasting and Predictive Analytics:

Another critical goal of sales metrics implementation is to enable organizations to leverage data-driven insights for forecasting and predictive analytics. By analyzing historical sales data, market trends, and customer behavior patterns, organizations can develop accurate sales forecasts and projections. These forecasts serve as valuable inputs for resource planning, inventory management, and strategic decision-making, enabling organizations to anticipate demand fluctuations, mitigate risks, and capitalize on emerging opportunities. Moreover, predictive analytics empowers organizations to identify early indicators of future performance trends, enabling proactive interventions to optimize sales outcomes and maximize revenue generation.

Process Optimization and Continuous Improvement:

Sales metrics implementation aims to drive process optimization and continuous improvement within sales operations. By systematically tracking and analyzing sales metrics, organizations can identify inefficiencies, bottlenecks, and areas for optimization within their sales processes. This enables targeted interventions to streamline workflows, eliminate redundant tasks, and enhance operational efficiency. Furthermore, sales metrics serve as a basis for performance feedback and coaching, enabling sales managers to provide actionable insights and support to their teams. This focus on continuous improvement fosters a culture of innovation, adaptability, and excellence, driving sustained growth and competitiveness.

Customer Insights and Relationship Management:

Sales metrics implementation facilitates the generation of valuable customer insights that inform effective relationship management strategies. By analyzing customer acquisition costs, lifetime value, and satisfaction metrics, organizations can identify high-value customer segments, prioritize relationship-building efforts, and tailor personalized sales approaches. Additionally, sales metrics enable organizations to track customer engagement levels, identify cross-selling and upselling opportunities, and anticipate evolving customer needs and preferences. This customer-centric approach enhances customer retention, loyalty, and advocacy, driving long-term revenue growth and profitability.

Risk Management and Compliance:

Effective sales metrics implementation supports proactive risk management and compliance initiatives within organizations. By monitoring key risk indicators such as sales pipeline health, sales cycle length, and win/loss ratios, organizations can identify potential risks and vulnerabilities in their sales operations. This enables preemptive actions to mitigate risks, such as addressing gaps in sales processes, implementing robust controls, and enhancing training and compliance programs. Furthermore, sales metrics help ensure regulatory compliance by tracking adherence to industry standards, ethical guidelines, and legal requirements, safeguarding organizational reputation and integrity.

In conclusion, the goals of sales metrics implementation encompass a broad spectrum of strategic objectives aimed at optimizing sales performance, driving revenue growth, and mitigating risks. By systematically evaluating performance, setting clear goals, leveraging predictive analytics, optimizing processes, and prioritizing customer relationships, organizations can enhance their competitive positioning and achieve sustainable business success in dynamic and challenging market environments.

CHAPTER I: INTRODUCTION

1.2 Importance of Tracking Performance for Growth

1.2.1 Impact on Revenue Generation

Tracking performance within sales operations is essential for driving sustainable growth and success in today's competitive business landscape. In this section, we explore the significance of tracking performance, with a specific focus on its impact on revenue generation. By comprehensively understanding how performance tracking influences revenue generation, organizations can optimize their sales strategies, maximize revenue streams, and achieve long-term business growth objectives.

Impact on Revenue Generation

Revenue generation lies at the core of every business's objectives, and effective performance tracking is instrumental in achieving revenue targets and sustaining growth momentum. Here, we delve into the various ways in which tracking performance directly influences revenue generation:

Identifying High-Performing Sales Channels and Strategies:

Performance tracking enables organizations to identify high-performing sales channels, marketing campaigns, and customer acquisition strategies. By analyzing key metrics such as conversion rates, customer acquisition costs, and revenue per channel, organizations can determine which sales channels and strategies yield the highest returns on investment. This insight allows for the allocation of resources towards the most lucrative opportunities, optimizing revenue generation efforts.

Optimizing Sales Processes and Conversion Rates:

Effective performance tracking provides visibility into the efficiency and effectiveness of sales processes, enabling organizations to identify and address bottlenecks and inefficiencies that may impede revenue generation. By analyzing metrics such as sales cycle length, lead response times, and opportunity-to-close ratios, organizations can streamline sales processes, shorten sales cycles, and increase conversion rates. This optimization of sales processes directly translates into accelerated revenue generation and improved sales performance.

Forecasting Revenue Trends and Projections:

Performance tracking facilitates accurate forecasting of revenue trends and projections by analyzing historical sales data, market trends, and customer behavior patterns. By leveraging predictive analytics models and forecasting tools, organizations can anticipate demand fluctuations, identify growth opportunities, and align sales strategies accordingly. This proactive approach to revenue forecasting enables organizations to capitalize on emerging market trends, mitigate revenue risks, and optimize resource allocation for maximum revenue generation.

Enhancing Customer Relationship Management:

Performance tracking plays a crucial role in enhancing customer relationship management (CRM) strategies, which are instrumental in driving revenue generation. By analyzing customer engagement metrics, purchase history, and satisfaction scores, organizations can personalize sales and marketing efforts, nurture customer relationships, and maximize customer lifetime value. Moreover, performance tracking enables organizations to identify cross-selling and upselling opportunities, further boosting revenue generation from existing customer bases.

Monitoring Sales Pipeline Health and Opportunities:

Performance tracking provides real-time visibility into the health of the sales pipeline, enabling organizations to monitor the progress of opportunities and identify potential revenue-generating prospects. By tracking metrics such as pipeline velocity, deal stage progression, and win/loss ratios, organizations can prioritize sales efforts, allocate resources effectively, and focus on high-probability opportunities. This proactive management of the sales pipeline ensures a steady influx of revenue and minimizes revenue leakage due to missed opportunities or stalled deals.

Measuring Return on Investment (ROI) and Profitability:

Performance tracking allows organizations to measure the return on investment (ROI) and profitability of sales and marketing initiatives, enabling informed decision-making and resource allocation. By analyzing metrics such as cost per acquisition, customer lifetime value, and marketing attribution, organizations can assess the effectiveness of various revenue-generating activities and optimize their investment strategies accordingly. This focus on ROI-driven decision-making ensures that resources are allocated to initiatives with the highest revenue-generating potential, maximizing overall profitability.

In summary, tracking performance is critical for driving revenue generation and sustaining business growth. By identifying high-performing sales channels, optimizing sales processes, forecasting revenue trends, enhancing customer relationship management, monitoring the sales pipeline, and measuring ROI and profitability, organizations can maximize their revenue streams and achieve long-term success in competitive markets. Effective performance tracking serves as a catalyst for revenue growth, enabling organizations to capitalize on opportunities, mitigate risks, and achieve their business objectives.

1.2.2 Enhancing Operational Efficiency

In addition to driving revenue generation, tracking performance within sales operations is instrumental in enhancing operational efficiency. Efficient sales processes are essential for maximizing productivity, minimizing costs, and optimizing resource utilization, ultimately contributing to overall business growth. In this section, we explore the importance of tracking performance for enhancing operational efficiency and achieving sustainable growth objectives.

Streamlining Sales Processes

Performance tracking enables organizations to identify inefficiencies and streamline sales processes for improved operational efficiency. By analyzing key metrics such as sales cycle length, lead response times, and time-to-close, organizations can pinpoint areas of process bottlenecks or redundancy. This insight allows for the implementation of targeted interventions to streamline workflows, eliminate unnecessary steps, and accelerate the sales cycle. Streamlining sales processes not only increases productivity but also enhances the overall customer experience by reducing wait times and improving responsiveness.

Resource Allocation Optimization

Tracking performance provides valuable insights for optimizing resource allocation within sales operations. By analyzing sales metrics such as sales rep productivity, territory performance, and conversion rates, organizations can allocate resources—such as sales personnel, marketing budgets, and technological investments—more effectively. This ensures that resources are directed towards high-potential opportunities and priority areas, maximizing ROI and minimizing wastage. Additionally, performance tracking enables organizations to adjust resource allocation dynamically in response to changing market conditions or business priorities, ensuring agility and adaptability in resource management.

Improving Sales Forecast Accuracy

Accurate sales forecasting is essential for effective resource planning and operational efficiency. Performance tracking allows organizations to analyze historical sales data, market trends, and customer behavior patterns to develop more accurate sales forecasts and projections. By leveraging predictive analytics models and forecasting tools, organizations can anticipate demand fluctuations, identify seasonal trends, and align resource allocation accordingly. This ensures that resources are allocated optimally to meet anticipated demand levels, minimizing underutilization or overextension of resources and enhancing operational efficiency.

Enhancing Sales Team Performance

Performance tracking serves as a valuable tool for enhancing sales team performance and productivity. By monitoring individual and team-level metrics such as sales quotas, conversion rates, and activity levels, organizations can identify top performers, as well as areas for improvement or development. This insight allows for targeted coaching, training, and performance management initiatives to maximize the effectiveness of the sales team. Additionally, performance tracking fosters a culture of accountability and transparency, where individuals take ownership of their targets and results, further enhancing overall sales team performance.

Identifying Training and Development Needs

Tracking performance provides organizations with actionable insights into the training and development needs of their sales teams. By analyzing performance metrics, organizations can identify skill gaps, knowledge deficiencies, and areas for improvement among sales personnel. This enables targeted training and development initiatives to address specific needs and enhance competencies. Additionally, performance tracking allows organizations to evaluate the effectiveness of training programs by measuring improvements in performance metrics over time, ensuring that training investments deliver tangible returns in terms of enhanced operational efficiency and sales effectiveness.

Implementing Process Automation and Technology Solutions

Performance tracking facilitates the identification of opportunities for process automation and the adoption of technology solutions to streamline sales operations. By analyzing workflow inefficiencies and repetitive tasks, organizations can identify opportunities for automation, such as lead scoring, email automation, and CRM integration. Implementing process automation not only increases operational efficiency by reducing manual workload and human error but also frees up valuable time and resources that can be redirected towards higher-value activities, such as strategic planning and customer relationship management.

In conclusion, tracking performance within sales operations is instrumental in enhancing operational efficiency and driving sustainable business growth. By streamlining sales processes, optimizing resource allocation, improving sales forecast accuracy, enhancing sales team performance, identifying training and development needs, and implementing process automation and technology solutions, organizations can maximize productivity, minimize costs, and optimize resource utilization. This focus on operational efficiency not only improves the bottom line but also strengthens competitiveness and facilitates long-term success in dynamic and challenging market environments.

CHAPTER II
Understanding Sales Metrics

2.1 Definition and Types of Sales Metrics

2.1.1 Leading vs. Lagging Indicators

In the realm of sales metrics, understanding the distinction between leading and lagging indicators is crucial for effective decision-making and performance evaluation. Both types of indicators offer valuable insights into the health and trajectory of a sales operation, yet they do so from different vantage points in the timeline of a sales cycle.

Leading Indicators

Leading indicators are predictive metrics that provide early signals of future performance trends. Unlike lagging indicators, which reflect past outcomes, leading indicators are forward-looking and proactive. They offer sales teams the opportunity to anticipate challenges, identify opportunities, and adjust strategies before the effects are fully realized. Let's delve into some common examples of leading indicators:

1. Sales Pipeline Velocity

Sales pipeline velocity measures the speed at which prospects move through the sales pipeline. It encompasses metrics such as the average time a lead spends in each stage of the sales process, the conversion rate between stages, and the overall length of the sales cycle. By analyzing pipeline velocity, sales teams can identify bottlenecks, optimize processes, and forecast future revenue with greater accuracy.

2. Activity-to-Outcome Ratios

Activity-to-outcome ratios assess the correlation between sales activities (e.g., calls, emails, meetings) and desired outcomes (e.g., conversions, closed deals). These ratios enable sales managers to evaluate the effectiveness of different outreach strategies, allocate resources efficiently, and coach representatives on high-impact behaviors. For instance, if a particular salesperson achieves a high conversion rate from email outreach compared to phone calls, the team may reallocate resources to prioritize email campaigns.

3. Lead Response Time

Lead response time measures the speed at which sales representatives respond to inbound leads or inquiries. Research indicates that the likelihood of qualifying a lead decreases significantly as response time increases. Therefore, minimizing response time is critical for maximizing lead conversion rates and enhancing the overall customer experience. Leading organizations often leverage automation tools, such as chatbots or lead routing software, to ensure rapid and personalized responses to incoming leads.

Lagging Indicators

Lagging indicators, in contrast to leading indicators, reflect historical performance outcomes. They provide a retrospective view of past activities and serve as benchmarks for evaluating success or failure. While lagging indicators are valuable for assessing the impact of previous strategies and initiatives, they offer limited insights into future trends or potential challenges. Here are some common examples of lagging indicators:

1. Sales Revenue

Sales revenue, perhaps the most fundamental metric in any sales organization, represents the total amount of money generated from product or service sales over a specific period. While sales revenue is a key performance indicator (KPI) for assessing financial health and growth, it provides little insight into the underlying factors driving revenue fluctuations. Therefore, sales leaders often complement revenue metrics with leading indicators to gain a more holistic understanding of sales performance.

2. Win Rate

The win rate measures the percentage of sales opportunities that result in closed deals. While win rate is an essential metric for evaluating sales effectiveness and efficiency, it does not reveal why certain opportunities were won or lost. To dissect the underlying reasons behind win rates, sales teams may conduct win-loss analyses, gathering feedback from customers and analyzing competitor strategies to inform future sales tactics.

3. Customer Satisfaction Scores

Customer satisfaction scores (CSAT) assess the level of satisfaction or dissatisfaction among customers regarding their interactions with a company's products, services, or support channels. While CSAT scores provide valuable feedback on customer sentiment and loyalty, they reflect historical experiences rather than predictive indicators of future behavior. To proactively address customer needs and enhance satisfaction levels, organizations often complement CSAT metrics with leading indicators such as Net Promoter Score (NPS) or customer feedback surveys conducted at various touchpoints throughout the customer journey.

Conclusion

In summary, leading and lagging indicators play complementary roles in the evaluation and optimization of sales performance. While leading indicators offer predictive insights to guide proactive decision-making and strategy refinement, lagging indicators provide retrospective benchmarks for assessing past outcomes and identifying areas for improvement. By leveraging a balanced combination of both types of indicators, sales organizations can achieve greater agility, efficiency, and success in today's competitive marketplace.

2.1.2 Revenue Metrics

Revenue metrics are essential tools for evaluating the financial performance and growth trajectory of a sales organization. By tracking various revenue-related indicators, businesses can assess the effectiveness of their sales strategies, identify areas for improvement, and make informed decisions to drive sustainable revenue growth. In this section, we will explore some key revenue metrics commonly used in sales analytics:

1. Gross Revenue

Gross revenue, also known as total revenue or gross sales, represents the total income generated from the sale of goods or services before deducting any expenses or costs. It provides a broad overview of a company's revenue-generating activities over a specific period. While gross revenue is a fundamental metric for assessing top-line growth, it does not account for operating expenses, taxes, or other deductions, making it an incomplete measure of profitability.

2. Net Revenue

Net revenue, sometimes referred to as net sales or net income, reflects the total revenue generated after subtracting discounts, returns, allowances, and any other deductions from gross revenue. Unlike gross revenue, which represents the total amount of money flowing into the business, net revenue provides a more accurate depiction of a company's financial health by accounting for factors that impact the bottom line. Monitoring net revenue trends allows businesses to evaluate their pricing strategies, customer retention efforts, and overall revenue optimization initiatives.

3. Average Revenue Per User (ARPU)

Average Revenue Per User (ARPU) calculates the average amount of revenue generated per customer or user within a specified timeframe. ARPU is particularly valuable for subscription-based businesses, SaaS (Software as a Service) companies, telecommunications providers, and other industries where recurring revenue plays a significant role. By tracking ARPU metrics, organizations can assess customer value, segment their customer base, and tailor their sales and marketing strategies to maximize revenue generation from different customer segments.

4. Average Deal Size

Average deal size, also known as average order value (AOV) or average transaction value (ATV), measures the average monetary value of individual sales transactions. Calculated by dividing total revenue by the number of deals closed within a specific period, average deal size provides insights into the typical size and scope of sales opportunities. Monitoring changes in average deal size over time can indicate shifts in customer purchasing behavior, the effectiveness of upselling or cross-selling initiatives, and the impact of pricing strategies on sales performance.

5. Revenue Growth Rate

Revenue growth rate quantifies the percentage increase or decrease in revenue over a given period, typically on a year-over-year (YoY) basis. It is a critical metric for assessing the pace of revenue expansion and overall business growth. Positive revenue growth signifies increasing demand for products or services, successful market penetration, and effective sales execution. Conversely, negative revenue growth may signal market saturation, competitive pressures, or operational challenges that require attention. Analyzing revenue growth trends enables businesses to adjust their sales strategies, allocate resources strategically, and capitalize on emerging opportunities in the marketplace.

Conclusion

In conclusion, revenue metrics are indispensable tools for monitoring the financial performance and viability of a sales organization. By tracking key revenue indicators such as gross revenue, net revenue, ARPU, average deal size, and revenue growth rate, businesses can gain valuable insights into their revenue-generating activities, identify areas for improvement, and drive sustainable growth. By incorporating revenue metrics into their sales analytics toolkit, companies can make data-driven decisions to optimize sales performance, enhance profitability, and achieve long-term success in today's competitive business landscape.

2.1.3 Activity Metrics

Activity metrics play a crucial role in sales performance evaluation by measuring the quantity and quality of sales-related actions undertaken by representatives and teams. Unlike revenue metrics, which focus on financial outcomes, activity metrics provide insights into the behaviors, efforts, and productivity levels of sales professionals. By tracking and analyzing activity metrics, organizations can assess sales effectiveness, identify areas for improvement, and optimize resource allocation to drive better results. In this section, we will explore various types of activity metrics commonly used in sales analytics:

1. Calls Made

The number of calls made measures the volume of outbound calls initiated by sales representatives to prospects, leads, or existing customers. Tracking call activity provides insights into sales team productivity, outreach efforts, and the effectiveness of call campaigns. Additionally, analyzing call metrics allows managers to identify top performers, coach representatives on call techniques, and optimize call scripts for better engagement and conversion rates.

2. Emails Sent

Email activity metrics quantify the number of emails sent by sales professionals as part of their outreach efforts. This metric encompasses both personalized emails and automated email campaigns targeted at different segments of the audience. By monitoring email activity, sales managers can evaluate the consistency and frequency of communication with prospects, assess the performance of email templates and subject lines, and refine email marketing strategies to improve open rates, click-through rates, and conversions.

3. Meetings Scheduled

Meetings scheduled measures the number of appointments or meetings arranged by sales representatives with prospects or clients. This metric indicates the effectiveness of lead nurturing efforts, the ability to qualify leads, and the success of sales outreach in driving meaningful interactions. Analyzing meeting activity allows sales managers to identify opportunities for pipeline acceleration, prioritize high-value prospects, and allocate resources strategically to maximize sales productivity and conversion rates.

4. Demos or Presentations Delivered

Demos or presentations delivered track the number of product demonstrations, sales presentations, or pitches delivered by sales professionals to showcase the features, benefits, and value proposition of their offerings. This metric reflects the depth of engagement with prospects, the level of interest generated, and the effectiveness of sales presentations in moving prospects through the sales funnel. By evaluating demo activity, sales teams can refine their presentation skills, tailor messaging to specific audience needs, and address objections more effectively to close deals successfully.

5. Proposals Submitted

Proposals submitted measures the number of formal proposals or quotes presented to prospects outlining the terms, pricing, and scope of proposed solutions. This metric indicates the level of interest and commitment from prospects, as well as the sales team's ability to effectively communicate value and address customer requirements. Analyzing proposal activity enables sales managers to assess deal progression, identify potential roadblocks or objections, and refine proposal templates or pricing strategies to improve win rates and deal velocity.

6. Follow-Up Actions Taken

Follow-up actions taken measure the efforts made by sales representatives to engage with prospects or leads after initial interactions. This includes activities such as sending follow-up emails, making follow-up calls, or conducting additional meetings to address questions or concerns. Tracking follow-up activity is crucial for nurturing relationships, building rapport, and moving prospects closer to a purchasing decision. By monitoring follow-up actions, sales teams can ensure consistent communication, demonstrate responsiveness, and reinforce value propositions to increase conversion rates and customer satisfaction.

7. Social Media Engagement

Social media engagement metrics quantify the level of interaction and audience response generated by sales professionals on various social media platforms. This includes metrics such as likes, comments, shares, and direct messages received on posts or content shared by sales representatives. Social media engagement provides insights into brand visibility, audience engagement, and the effectiveness of social selling efforts in building relationships and generating leads. By analyzing social media metrics, sales teams can identify content preferences, tailor messaging to resonate with target audiences, and leverage social networks to expand their reach and influence.

8. Networking Events Attended

Networking events attended measure the participation of sales professionals in industry conferences, trade shows, seminars, and other networking opportunities. This metric reflects the proactive efforts of sales representatives to build connections, expand their professional network, and generate leads through face-to-face interactions. Attending networking events allows sales professionals to establish credibility, gain industry insights, and identify potential prospects or referral partners. By tracking event attendance and measuring subsequent lead generation or business opportunities, sales managers can evaluate the effectiveness of networking strategies and allocate resources to events with the highest return on investment (ROI).

9. Training and Development Activities

Training and development activities metrics assess the level of investment and engagement in ongoing learning and skill development initiatives by sales professionals. This includes participation in sales training programs, workshops, webinars, and self-paced learning modules designed to enhance product knowledge, sales techniques, and soft skills. Monitoring training and development activities allows organizations to ensure continuous improvement, upskill sales teams to meet evolving market demands, and foster a culture of learning and professional growth. By tracking training metrics, sales managers can identify skills gaps, tailor training programs to address specific needs, and empower sales representatives to perform at their best.

10. Time Management Metrics

Time management metrics evaluate how sales professionals allocate their time across different activities and priorities. This includes metrics such as time spent on prospecting, lead qualification, client meetings, administrative tasks, and professional development. Effective time management is essential for maximizing productivity, maintaining focus, and achieving sales targets. By analyzing time management metrics, sales managers can identify inefficiencies, streamline workflows, and provide targeted coaching or support to help sales representatives optimize their time and prioritize high-impact activities that drive results.

Conclusion

In summary, activity metrics provide valuable insights into the behaviors, efforts, and productivity levels of sales professionals, enabling organizations to assess sales effectiveness, identify areas for improvement, and optimize sales strategies for better outcomes. By tracking metrics such as follow-up actions taken, social media engagement, networking events attended, training and development activities, and time management, businesses can empower their sales teams to perform at their best, drive revenue growth, and achieve sustainable success in today's competitive marketplace. Incorporating activity metrics into sales performance evaluation processes fosters accountability, transparency, and continuous improvement, ultimately leading to enhanced sales performance and customer satisfaction.

2.2 Key Performance Indicators (KPIs) in Sales

2.2.1 Customer Acquisition Cost (CAC)

Customer Acquisition Cost (CAC) is a critical metric that quantifies the amount of money a company spends to acquire a new customer. Understanding and effectively managing CAC is essential for optimizing sales and marketing strategies, maximizing profitability, and achieving sustainable growth. In this section, we will delve into the definition, calculation, significance, and strategies for managing CAC effectively.

Definition of Customer Acquisition Cost (CAC)

Customer Acquisition Cost (CAC) is the total cost incurred by a company to acquire a new customer within a specific period, typically measured in months or years. This metric encompasses all expenses related to sales and marketing activities aimed at attracting, engaging, and converting prospects into paying customers. These expenses may include advertising costs, sales team salaries and commissions, marketing campaigns, lead generation expenses, technology and software investments, and any other direct costs associated with customer acquisition efforts.

Calculation of Customer Acquisition Cost (CAC)

The formula for calculating Customer Acquisition Cost (CAC) is straightforward:

CAC = Total Sales and Marketing Expenses / Number of New Customers Acquired

For example, if a company spends $100,000 on sales and marketing efforts in a given month and acquires 100 new customers during the same period, the CAC would be calculated as follows:

CAC = $100,000/100 = $1,000

This means that on average, the company spent $1,000 to acquire each new customer during that month.

Significance of Customer Acquisition Cost (CAC)

Understanding CAC is crucial for several reasons:

1. Profitability Analysis: CAC helps businesses determine the effectiveness of their sales and marketing investments in relation to the revenue generated from new customers. By comparing CAC to customer lifetime value (CLV), companies can assess whether their customer acquisition efforts are yielding positive returns and contributing to overall profitability.

2. Resource Allocation: CAC insights inform resource allocation decisions, enabling companies to allocate their sales and marketing budgets effectively. By identifying the most cost-effective channels and strategies for customer acquisition, businesses can optimize their investment to achieve maximum results.

3. Performance Measurement: CAC serves as a key performance indicator (KPI) for evaluating the efficiency and effectiveness of sales and marketing initiatives. Monitoring CAC trends over time allows companies to assess the impact of changes in strategy, pricing, targeting, or market conditions on customer acquisition costs.

4. Forecasting and Planning: CAC data provides valuable insights for forecasting future sales and marketing expenses, setting budgetary targets, and developing strategic plans for scaling customer acquisition efforts. By projecting CAC based on historical data and market trends, businesses can make informed decisions to support growth objectives.

Strategies for Managing Customer Acquisition Cost (CAC)

To manage CAC effectively and optimize customer acquisition efforts, businesses can implement the following strategies:

1. Targeted Marketing: Focus on identifying and targeting the most profitable customer segments through personalized marketing campaigns, segmentation strategies, and targeted messaging that resonates with the needs and preferences of ideal customers.

2. Lead Qualification: Implement robust lead qualification processes to ensure that sales and marketing resources are allocated to prospects with the highest likelihood of conversion. By prioritizing qualified leads, businesses can minimize wasted resources and improve conversion rates, thereby reducing CAC.

3. Conversion Rate Optimization: Continuously optimize conversion funnels, sales processes, and marketing channels to improve conversion rates and maximize the efficiency of customer acquisition efforts. A/B testing, website optimization, and sales enablement tools can help identify and implement improvements to enhance conversion rates and reduce CAC.

4. Customer Retention: Invest in customer retention strategies and initiatives to enhance customer loyalty, increase lifetime value, and reduce the need for constant acquisition efforts. Providing exceptional customer service, offering loyalty programs, and fostering long-term relationships can lower CAC by maximizing the revenue generated from existing customers.

5. Efficiency Improvements: Identify opportunities to streamline sales and marketing operations, automate repetitive tasks, and leverage technology solutions to improve efficiency and reduce overhead costs associated with customer acquisition. Implementing marketing automation platforms, CRM systems, and sales productivity tools can enhance workflow efficiency and lower CAC.

Conclusion

In conclusion, Customer Acquisition Cost (CAC) is a critical metric that provides insights into the cost-effectiveness and efficiency of customer acquisition efforts. By understanding CAC, businesses can assess the impact of sales and marketing investments on profitability, allocate resources effectively, measure performance, and develop strategies for optimizing customer acquisition processes. By implementing targeted marketing, lead qualification, conversion rate optimization, customer retention, and efficiency improvement strategies, companies can manage CAC effectively and drive sustainable growth in today's competitive marketplace. Tracking CAC alongside other key metrics such as customer lifetime value (CLV) and sales conversion rate enables businesses to make data-driven decisions, achieve better results, and ultimately, maximize long-term success and profitability.

2.2.2 Customer Lifetime Value (CLV)

Customer Lifetime Value (CLV) is a fundamental metric in sales and marketing that measures the total revenue a business can expect from a single customer throughout their entire relationship with the company. Understanding and effectively managing CLV is essential for maximizing customer profitability, guiding strategic decision-making, and driving sustainable growth. In this section, we will explore the definition, calculation, significance, and strategies for optimizing Customer Lifetime Value (CLV).

Definition of Customer Lifetime Value (CLV)

Customer Lifetime Value (CLV), also known as Lifetime Customer Value (LCV) or Lifetime Value (LTV), represents the net profit attributed to the entire future relationship with a customer. It takes into account all potential revenue streams, including repeat purchases, upsells, cross-sells, referrals, and subscription renewals, over the customer's lifetime. CLV provides a comprehensive view of customer value beyond just the initial transaction, allowing businesses to prioritize customer acquisition and retention efforts based on long-term profitability.

Calculation of Customer Lifetime Value (CLV)

There are various methods for calculating Customer Lifetime Value (CLV), with the simplest approach being:

$$CLV = \text{Average Revenue per Customer} / \text{Churn Rate}$$

Alternatively, a more comprehensive formula for calculating CLV is:

$$CLV = [\text{Average Revenue per Customer} \times \text{Gross Margin \%}] / \text{Churn Rate}$$

Where:

- Average Revenue per Customer: The average amount of revenue generated from a customer over their lifetime.

- Gross Margin %: The percentage of revenue that represents gross profit after accounting for the cost of goods sold (COGS).

- Churn Rate: The rate at which customers cease their relationship with the company or stop purchasing.

Significance of Customer Lifetime Value (CLV)

Understanding CLV is crucial for several reasons:

1. Customer Segmentation: CLV enables businesses to segment their customer base based on value and profitability. By identifying high-value customers, businesses can tailor marketing strategies, service offerings, and communication channels to maximize retention and revenue generation from these segments.

2. Resource Allocation: CLV insights inform resource allocation decisions, allowing businesses to invest resources strategically in acquiring and retaining high-value customers. By focusing marketing and sales efforts on customers with the highest lifetime value potential, businesses can optimize ROI and profitability.

3. Retention Strategies: CLV highlights the importance of customer retention as a driver of long-term profitability. By understanding the factors that contribute to customer churn and implementing retention strategies, such as loyalty programs, personalized communication, and exceptional customer service, businesses can extend customer lifetimes and maximize CLV.

4. Cross-Selling and Upselling: CLV analysis identifies opportunities for cross-selling and upselling additional products or services to existing customers. By understanding customer preferences, purchase patterns, and lifetime value potential, businesses can develop targeted upselling and cross-selling strategies to increase revenue per customer and enhance CLV.

Strategies for Optimizing Customer Lifetime Value (CLV)

To optimize Customer Lifetime Value (CLV) and maximize long-term profitability, businesses can implement the following strategies:

1. **Enhanced Customer Experience:** Focus on delivering exceptional customer experiences at every touchpoint throughout the customer journey. By providing personalized service, addressing customer needs proactively, and exceeding expectations, businesses can foster loyalty, increase customer satisfaction, and extend customer lifetimes.

2. **Retention Marketing:** Implement targeted retention marketing strategies to engage and retain existing customers. This includes personalized email campaigns, loyalty programs, exclusive offers, and proactive communication to nurture relationships and encourage repeat purchases.

3. **Product and Service Expansion:** Continuously innovate and expand product or service offerings to meet evolving customer needs and preferences. By diversifying offerings, businesses can increase cross-selling and upselling opportunities, encourage repeat purchases, and enhance overall customer lifetime value.

4. **Predictive Analytics**: Utilize data analytics and predictive modeling techniques to forecast future customer behavior, identify at-risk customers, and intervene proactively to prevent churn. By leveraging customer data and insights, businesses can anticipate needs, personalize offerings, and optimize retention efforts to maximize CLV.

5. **Customer Relationship Management (CRM):** Implement a robust CRM system to centralize customer data, track interactions, and manage relationships effectively. By leveraging CRM tools, businesses can segment customers based on CLV, track customer engagement, and tailor communication and marketing efforts to maximize CLV and retention.

Conclusion

In conclusion, Customer Lifetime Value (CLV) is a key metric that quantifies the long-term revenue potential of a customer and informs strategic decision-making in sales and marketing. By understanding CLV and implementing strategies to optimize customer relationships, businesses can maximize profitability, drive sustainable growth, and build a loyal customer base. By focusing on delivering exceptional customer experiences, implementing retention marketing strategies, expanding product offerings, leveraging predictive analytics, and utilizing CRM systems effectively, businesses can enhance CLV and achieve long-term success in today's competitive marketplace. Tracking CLV alongside other key performance indicators (KPIs) enables businesses to make data-driven decisions, prioritize investments, and allocate resources to maximize customer lifetime value and drive sustainable business growth.

2.2.3 Sales Conversion Rate

Sales Conversion Rate is a crucial Key Performance Indicator (KPI) in sales that measures the effectiveness of converting prospects or leads into paying customers. Understanding and optimizing the sales conversion rate is essential for maximizing revenue generation, improving sales efficiency, and achieving sustainable growth. In this section, we will explore the definition, calculation, significance, and strategies for optimizing the Sales Conversion Rate.

Definition of Sales Conversion Rate

Sales Conversion Rate, often simply referred to as Conversion Rate, is the percentage of leads or prospects that successfully transition through the sales funnel and complete a desired action, such as making a purchase, signing a contract, or subscribing to a service. It measures the efficiency of the sales process in turning leads into customers and indicates the effectiveness of sales strategies, techniques, and tactics employed by the sales team.

Calculation of Sales Conversion Rate

The formula for calculating Sales Conversion Rate is straightforward:

Conversion Rate = [Number of Conversion / Number of Leads or Prospects] x 100%

For example, if a sales team generates 100 leads in a month and closes 20 of them as paying customers, the Sales Conversion Rate would be calculated as follows:

Conversion Rate = (20/100) x 100% = 20%

This means that 20% of the leads generated were successfully converted into customers during that period.

Significance of Sales Conversion Rate

Sales Conversion Rate is significant for several reasons:

1. Performance Measurement: Conversion Rate serves as a key performance indicator (KPI) for evaluating the effectiveness of sales efforts and strategies. It provides insights into the success of lead generation, qualification, and nurturing processes, as well as the ability of sales representatives to close deals and generate revenue.

2. Revenue Generation: Improving the Conversion Rate directly impacts revenue generation by increasing the number of customers acquired from a given pool of leads. By optimizing the sales process and improving conversion efficiency, businesses can boost sales performance and drive revenue growth without necessarily increasing marketing spend.

3. Sales Pipeline Optimization: Conversion Rate analysis helps identify bottlenecks and inefficiencies in the sales pipeline, enabling businesses to streamline processes, remove obstacles, and accelerate the pace of lead progression. By understanding conversion rates at each stage of the sales funnel, organizations can focus resources on areas that have the greatest potential for improvement.

4. Customer Insights: Conversion Rate data provides valuable insights into customer behavior, preferences, and needs. By analyzing conversion patterns and trends, businesses can identify common characteristics among high-converting leads, tailor messaging and offerings to better align with customer needs, and refine targeting strategies for improved results.

Strategies for Optimizing Sales Conversion Rate

To optimize Sales Conversion Rate and improve overall sales performance, businesses can implement the following strategies:

1. Targeted Lead Generation: Focus on attracting high-quality leads that are more likely to convert into customers. Utilize targeted marketing campaigns, personalized messaging, and audience segmentation to reach prospects who match the ideal customer profile and are more likely to have a genuine interest in the product or service offered.

2. Effective Lead Nurturing: Implement a structured lead nurturing process to engage and educate leads throughout the buyer's journey. Provide valuable content, address pain points, and build trust with prospects through personalized communication and targeted follow-up strategies to guide them towards a purchasing decision.

3. Streamlined Sales Process: Simplify and optimize the sales process to reduce friction and eliminate barriers to conversion. Provide sales representatives with the necessary tools, resources, and training to effectively communicate value propositions, address objections, and guide prospects through the sales funnel with confidence and efficiency.

4. Continuous Improvement: Adopt a data-driven approach to sales optimization by monitoring and analyzing Conversion Rate data regularly. Identify areas for improvement, test different strategies and tactics, and iterate based on results to continuously refine the sales process and maximize conversion efficiency over time.

5. Customer-Centric Approach: Prioritize the needs and preferences of customers throughout the sales process. Listen actively, demonstrate empathy, and tailor solutions to meet customer requirements, ensuring a positive buying experience that fosters trust, loyalty, and long-term relationships.

Conclusion

In conclusion, Sales Conversion Rate is a critical metric that measures the efficiency of converting leads into customers and plays a key role in driving revenue growth and sales performance. By understanding the factors that influence conversion rates and implementing strategies to optimize the sales process, businesses can improve conversion efficiency, increase revenue generation, and achieve sustainable growth. By focusing on targeted lead generation, effective lead nurturing, streamlined sales processes, continuous improvement, and a customer-centric approach, organizations can maximize Sales Conversion Rate and enhance overall sales effectiveness in today's competitive marketplace. Tracking Conversion Rate alongside other key performance indicators (KPIs) enables businesses to make data-driven decisions, identify opportunities for improvement, and drive continuous sales optimization for long-term success and profitability.

2.3 Setting SMART Goals for Sales Metrics

Setting SMART (Specific, Measurable, Achievable, Relevant, Time-bound) goals is essential for guiding sales teams towards success and achieving desired outcomes. In this section, we will explore how to apply the SMART framework to sales metrics effectively, starting with setting specific goals.

2.3.1 Specific

Specific goals provide clarity and focus, ensuring that sales teams understand exactly what is expected of them and what they need to accomplish. When setting specific goals for sales metrics, it's important to define the desired outcome clearly and precisely.

Why Specific Goals Matter

1. Clarity: Specific goals eliminate ambiguity and provide clear direction to sales teams. When goals are specific, sales representatives know exactly what is expected of them and can align their efforts accordingly.

2. Focus: Specific goals help sales teams prioritize their activities and focus on tasks that contribute directly to achieving the desired outcome. By eliminating distractions and unnecessary tasks, sales representatives can maximize their efficiency and productivity.

3. Motivation: Clear, specific goals provide a sense of purpose and motivation for sales teams. When employees understand the importance of their objectives and how their efforts contribute to the overall success of the organization, they are more likely to be engaged and motivated to perform at their best.

How to Set Specific Goals for Sales Metrics

When setting specific goals for sales metrics, consider the following guidelines:

1. Define Clear Objectives: Clearly define the specific outcomes you want to achieve with your sales metrics. For example, if you're setting a goal for increasing revenue, specify the target revenue amount or percentage growth you aim to achieve within a certain timeframe.

2. Identify Key Metrics: Identify the specific sales metrics that align with your objectives and are most relevant to measuring success. Whether it's customer acquisition, revenue growth, or sales conversion rate, ensure that the chosen metrics are directly tied to your goals.

3. Set Quantifiable Targets: Make sure your goals are quantifiable and measurable, allowing you to track progress and evaluate success objectively. Instead of setting a vague goal like "increase revenue," set a specific target such as "increase monthly revenue by 10% within the next quarter."

4. Consider Context and Constraints: Take into account the context of your sales environment, including market conditions, industry trends, and internal capabilities. Ensure that your goals are realistic and achievable given the resources and constraints your sales team faces.

5. Communicate Clearly: Communicate the specific goals and objectives to your sales team clearly and effectively. Provide context, rationale, and expectations surrounding the goals to ensure alignment and understanding among team members.

Example of Setting Specific Goals for Sales Metrics

Let's consider an example of setting specific goals for the sales metric of customer acquisition:

General Goal: Increase customer acquisition.

Specific Goal: Increase the number of new customers acquired through digital marketing campaigns by 20% within the next six months.

Key Metrics:

- Number of new customers acquired through digital marketing campaigns.

- Conversion rate of digital marketing campaigns.

- Cost per acquisition (CPA) for digital marketing channels.

Context and Constraints:

- Consider current conversion rates and historical performance of digital marketing campaigns.

- Assess the budget and resources available for scaling digital marketing efforts.

- Take into account market trends and competitor activities in the digital marketing space.

Communication:

- Clearly communicate the specific goal, target metrics, and timeline to the digital marketing team.

- Provide support, resources, and guidance to help the team achieve the desired outcome.

- Monitor progress regularly and provide feedback and adjustments as needed.

By setting specific goals for sales metrics using the SMART framework, organizations can provide clear direction, focus, and motivation for their sales teams, ultimately driving performance and achieving desired outcomes.

2.3.2 Measurable

Measurable goals provide a quantifiable way to track progress and evaluate performance. When setting measurable goals for sales metrics, it's essential to establish clear criteria for success and define how progress will be assessed.

Why Measurable Goals Matter

1. Track Progress: Measurable goals allow sales teams to track their progress over time and assess whether they are on track to achieve their objectives. By measuring performance against specific targets, teams can identify areas for improvement and make data-driven decisions to drive results.

2. Identify Success: Measurable goals provide clarity on what success looks like and enable sales teams to celebrate achievements when milestones are reached. By defining clear metrics for success, teams have a tangible benchmark to strive for and can stay motivated throughout the process.

3. Focus Efforts: Measurable goals help sales teams prioritize their efforts and allocate resources effectively. By focusing on metrics that directly impact performance and align with business objectives, teams can optimize their strategies and maximize their impact on key outcomes.

How to Set Measurable Goals for Sales Metrics

When setting measurable goals for sales metrics, consider the following guidelines:

1. Define Specific Metrics: Clearly define the sales metrics that will be used to measure progress towards the goal. Whether it's revenue, number of new customers, sales conversion rate, or average deal size, ensure that the chosen metrics are relevant to the objective.

2. Set Quantifiable Targets: Establish specific targets or benchmarks that indicate success. Whether it's increasing revenue by a certain percentage, acquiring a specific number of new customers, or improving the sales conversion rate to a defined level, make sure the targets are quantifiable and measurable.

3. Choose Appropriate Measurement Tools: Select the tools and systems needed to accurately track and measure progress towards the goal. Whether it's a CRM platform, sales analytics software, or custom reporting tools, ensure that you have access to the necessary data and insights to monitor performance effectively.

4. Establish Reporting Cadence: Define how progress towards the goal will be monitored and reported. Whether it's weekly, monthly, or quarterly reporting, establish a cadence that allows for regular assessment of performance and enables timely adjustments to strategies and tactics.

5. Align with Business Objectives: Ensure that the measurable goals for sales metrics align with broader business objectives and priorities. By linking sales goals to overarching business goals, teams can ensure that their efforts are contributing directly to the success of the organization.

Example of Setting Measurable Goals for Sales Metrics

Let's consider an example of setting measurable goals for the sales metric of revenue:

General Goal: Increase revenue.

Measurable Goal: Increase monthly revenue by 15% compared to the previous quarter.

Key Metrics:

- Total monthly revenue.

- Revenue growth rate.

- Average deal size.

Quantifiable Targets:

- Achieve a total monthly revenue of $500,000 by the end of the quarter.

- Increase the revenue growth rate from 10% to 15%.

- Increase the average deal size from $5,000 to $6,000.

Measurement Tools:

- Utilize the company's CRM system to track revenue performance and trends.

- Implement sales analytics software to analyze revenue data and identify areas for improvement.

Reporting Cadence:

- Review revenue performance and progress towards targets on a monthly basis during sales team meetings.

- Provide quarterly reports to senior management and stakeholders to communicate progress towards revenue goals.

Alignment with Business Objectives:

- Increasing revenue aligns with the company's objective of achieving sustainable growth and profitability.

- The measurable targets for revenue growth directly contribute to achieving broader financial goals and objectives.

By setting measurable goals for sales metrics using the SMART framework, organizations can establish clear criteria for success, track progress effectively, and drive performance towards achieving desired outcomes. Measurable goals provide sales teams with a roadmap for success and enable them to focus their efforts on activities that have the greatest impact on driving results.

2.3.3 Achievable

Achievable goals are realistic and attainable within the constraints of the organization's resources, capabilities, and timeframe. When setting achievable goals for sales metrics, it's essential to consider factors such as available resources, market conditions, and historical performance.

Why Achievable Goals Matter

1. Motivation and Engagement: Achievable goals provide sales teams with a sense of confidence and motivation, knowing that the targets they are working towards are realistic and within reach. When goals are achievable, employees are more likely to stay engaged and committed to achieving them.

2. Resource Allocation: Setting achievable goals ensures that sales teams are not overburdened or stretched too thin, allowing for optimal resource allocation and utilization. By aligning goals with available resources and capabilities, organizations can set their teams up for success and avoid burnout.

3. Maintaining Momentum: Achievable goals help maintain momentum and progress towards larger objectives by breaking them down into manageable steps. By setting incremental, achievable targets, sales teams can make consistent progress over time, leading to sustainable growth and success.

How to Set Achievable Goals for Sales Metrics

When setting achievable goals for sales metrics, consider the following guidelines:

1. Assess Current Performance: Evaluate the organization's current performance and historical data to set realistic benchmarks for improvement. Consider factors such as past sales performance, market trends, and competitive landscape to gauge what is achievable within a given timeframe.

2. Consider Resources and Constraints: Take into account the resources, capabilities, and constraints of the organization when setting goals. Ensure that goals are aligned with available budget, manpower, technology, and other necessary resources to support sales efforts effectively.

3. Break Down Larger Goals: If the overall objective seems daunting, break it down into smaller, more achievable milestones or targets. By setting incremental goals, sales teams can make progress gradually and build momentum over time, leading to greater success in the long run.

4. Involve Key Stakeholders: Collaborate with key stakeholders, including sales managers, team leaders, and other relevant parties, when setting goals. By involving stakeholders in the goal-setting process, you can gain valuable insights, foster buy-in, and ensure that goals are realistic and achievable.

5. Monitor and Adjust: Continuously monitor progress towards goals and be prepared to adjust targets or strategies as needed. If circumstances change or unforeseen challenges arise, be flexible and adaptable in modifying goals to ensure they remain achievable and relevant.

Example of Setting Achievable Goals for Sales Metrics

Let's consider an example of setting achievable goals for the sales metric of customer acquisition:

General Goal: Increase customer acquisition.

Achievable Goal: Increase the number of new customers acquired by 10% compared to the previous quarter.

Considerations:

- Assess historical data to ensure that a 10% increase is feasible based on past performance.

- Determine if the sales team has the necessary resources, such as marketing support and lead generation tools, to support increased customer acquisition efforts.

- Break down the goal into specific action steps, such as increasing lead generation activities or improving conversion rates, to make it more achievable.

By setting achievable goals for sales metrics using the SMART framework, organizations can ensure that their sales teams are working towards targets that are realistic and within reach. Achievable goals provide motivation, maintain momentum, and facilitate progress towards broader business objectives, ultimately driving sales success and organizational growth.

2.3.4 Relevant

Relevant goals are aligned with the overall objectives and priorities of the organization. When setting relevant goals for sales metrics, it's crucial to ensure that they contribute directly to driving business growth and success.

Why Relevant Goals Matter

1. Alignment with Business Objectives: Relevant goals ensure that sales efforts are aligned with the broader objectives and priorities of the organization. By focusing on metrics that directly impact business growth, sales teams can contribute more effectively to overall success.

2. Maximizing Impact: Relevant goals help prioritize sales activities and resources towards initiatives that have the greatest impact on achieving desired outcomes. By concentrating efforts on areas that are most relevant to business objectives, sales teams can optimize their performance and drive meaningful results.

3. Motivation and Engagement: Relevant goals provide sales teams with a sense of purpose and motivation, knowing that their efforts are directly contributing to the success of the organization. When goals are relevant and meaningful, employees are more likely to stay engaged and committed to achieving them.

How to Set Relevant Goals for Sales Metrics

When setting relevant goals for sales metrics, consider the following guidelines:

1. Align with Business Objectives: Ensure that sales goals are directly aligned with the broader objectives and priorities of the organization. Whether it's increasing revenue, expanding market share, or improving customer satisfaction, make sure that sales metrics support these overarching goals.

2. Focus on Key Performance Indicators (KPIs): Identify the key performance indicators (KPIs) that are most relevant to measuring success in achieving business objectives. Whether it's customer acquisition, revenue growth, or sales conversion rate, prioritize metrics that have a direct impact on business outcomes.

3. Consider External Factors: Take into account external factors such as market conditions, industry trends, and competitive landscape when setting sales goals. Ensure that goals are relevant to the current business environment and adaptable to changes in the market.

4. Tailor Goals to Sales Teams: Customize goals to fit the specific needs and capabilities of different sales teams within the organization. Consider factors such as team size, geographic location, and target market when setting goals to ensure relevance and applicability.

5. Regularly Review and Adjust: Continuously monitor progress towards goals and be prepared to adjust them as needed based on changing circumstances or priorities. Regularly review sales metrics and performance data to ensure that goals remain relevant and aligned with business objectives.

Example of Setting Relevant Goals for Sales Metrics

Let's consider an example of setting relevant goals for the sales metric of customer acquisition:

General Business Objective: Increase market share in the target market.

Relevant Goal: Increase customer acquisition by 15% in the target market within the next fiscal year.

Considerations:

- Aligns with the broader objective of expanding market share.

- Directly contributes to business growth and revenue generation.

- Takes into account the specific needs and characteristics of the target market.

By setting relevant goals for sales metrics using the SMART framework, organizations can ensure that their sales efforts are aligned with broader business objectives and priorities. Relevant goals provide clarity, focus, and motivation for sales teams, ultimately driving performance and contributing to the overall success of the organization.

2.3.5 Time-bound

Time-bound goals have a defined timeline or deadline for achievement, providing a sense of urgency and accountability. When setting time-bound goals for sales metrics, it's essential to establish clear milestones and deadlines to drive progress and measure success.

Why Time-bound Goals Matter

1. Sense of Urgency: Time-bound goals create a sense of urgency and focus, motivating sales teams to take action and prioritize tasks to meet deadlines. By setting specific timelines for achievement, organizations can accelerate progress and maintain momentum towards their objectives.

2. Accountability: Establishing deadlines for goals enhances accountability and ensures that sales teams are held accountable for achieving results within a specified timeframe. By assigning clear deadlines, organizations can track progress effectively and take corrective action if necessary to stay on track.

3. Measurable Progress: Time-bound goals enable organizations to measure progress and performance over time, allowing for regular assessment of success and identification of areas for improvement. By breaking down larger goals into smaller, time-bound milestones, organizations can monitor progress more effectively and make data-driven decisions to drive success.

How to Set Time-bound Goals for Sales Metrics

When setting time-bound goals for sales metrics, consider the following guidelines:

1. Establish Clear Deadlines: Set specific deadlines or timelines for achieving sales goals, whether it's increasing revenue, acquiring new customers, or improving sales conversion rates. Define both short-term and long-term deadlines to create a roadmap for success.

2. Break Down Goals into Milestones: Divide larger goals into smaller, time-bound milestones or targets to track progress and maintain momentum. Establishing incremental deadlines allows sales teams to focus on achievable objectives and celebrate milestones along the way.

3. Consider Seasonality and Trends: Take into account seasonal variations, market trends, and other external factors when setting time-bound goals. Adjust deadlines and expectations accordingly to accommodate fluctuations in demand and market conditions.

4. Allocate Resources Appropriately: Ensure that sales teams have the necessary resources, support, and training to achieve time-bound goals effectively. Allocate resources strategically to support sales efforts and address any obstacles or challenges that may arise along the way.

5. Regularly Review and Adjust: Continuously monitor progress towards time-bound goals and be prepared to adjust deadlines or strategies as needed. Regularly review sales metrics and performance data to identify trends, evaluate effectiveness, and make timely adjustments to stay on track towards achieving objectives.

Example of Setting Time-bound Goals for Sales Metrics

Let's consider an example of setting time-bound goals for the sales metric of revenue:

General Goal: Increase annual revenue by 20%.

Time-bound Goal: Increase quarterly revenue by 5% over the next four quarters.

Considerations:

- Establishes a clear timeline for achieving the overall revenue target.

- Breaks down the larger goal into smaller, achievable milestones.

- Allows for regular assessment of progress and adjustment of strategies as needed.

By setting time-bound goals for sales metrics using the SMART framework, organizations can create a sense of urgency, accountability, and focus among sales teams. Time-bound goals provide a roadmap for success, enabling organizations to track progress effectively, maintain momentum, and achieve desired outcomes within specified deadlines.

Let's explore a specific example of setting SMART goals for sales metrics in a fictional company, ABC Corporation.

Example: ABC Corporation

Background:

ABC Corporation is a software-as-a-service (SaaS) company that provides a project management platform for small and medium-sized businesses. The company's sales team is looking to increase revenue and customer acquisition while improving overall sales performance.

Objective:

To increase annual revenue by 25% and acquire 100 new customers within the next fiscal year.

1. Specific:

- Specific Goal: Increase revenue and acquire new customers.

- Clarification: The goal is clearly defined, focusing on both revenue growth and customer acquisition, two key objectives for the sales team.

2. Measurable:

- Measurable Goal: Increase annual revenue by 25% and acquire 100 new customers.

- Metrics: Total revenue generated and the number of new customers acquired.

- Targets: Achieve $1,500,000 in total revenue (25% increase from the previous year) and acquire 100 new customers within the next fiscal year.

3. Achievable:

- Achievable Goal: Increase revenue and customer acquisition within the company's capabilities and resources.

- Assessment: Based on past performance and market analysis, a 25% revenue increase and acquiring 100 new customers are ambitious but realistic goals.

4. Relevant:

- Relevant Goal: Increasing revenue and customer acquisition directly contribute to the company's growth objectives.

- Alignment: These goals align with the company's overarching objectives of expanding its customer base and increasing profitability.

5. Time-bound:

- Time-bound Goal: Achieve the revenue and customer acquisition targets within the next fiscal year.

- Timeline: Goals are set for the next 12 months, providing a clear deadline for achievement.

Action Plan:

1. **Marketing Campaigns:** Launch targeted marketing campaigns to generate leads and attract new customers. Implement strategies such as email marketing, content marketing, and social media advertising.

2. **Sales Outreach:** Increase sales outreach efforts to engage with potential customers and convert leads into paying customers. Utilize cold calling, email outreach, and personalized demos to drive sales conversions.

3. **Customer Retention:** Focus on retaining existing customers by providing excellent customer service, ongoing support, and product enhancements. Enhancing customer satisfaction can lead to repeat business and referrals.

4. Sales Training: Provide sales team members with comprehensive training and resources to improve their selling skills and product knowledge. Invest in ongoing training programs to ensure that the sales team is equipped to meet targets effectively.

5. Performance Monitoring: Regularly monitor sales performance against targets and adjust strategies as needed. Utilize sales analytics tools and CRM systems to track progress, identify trends, and make data-driven decisions.

By setting SMART goals and implementing a strategic action plan, ABC Corporation can effectively drive sales performance, achieve revenue growth, and acquire new customers to support long-term business success.

Let's consider another example for setting SMART goals for sales metrics, this time for a retail company, XYZ Retail Inc.

Example: XYZ Retail Inc.

Background:

XYZ Retail Inc. is a multinational retail chain specializing in electronics and home appliances. The company aims to boost sales performance and enhance market share in its target regions.

Objective:

To increase quarterly sales revenue by 15% and improve the sales conversion rate by 20% within the next six months.

1. Specific:

- **Specific Goal:** Increase sales revenue and improve sales conversion rate.

- **Clarification:** The goal focuses on two specific areas of sales performance: revenue growth and conversion rate improvement, addressing key priorities for the company.

2. Measurable:

- **Measurable Goal:** Increase quarterly sales revenue by 15% and improve the sales conversion rate by 20%.

- **Metrics:** Total sales revenue generated and the percentage of leads converted into customers.

- **Targets:** Achieve $10 million in quarterly sales revenue (15% increase from the previous quarter) and increase the sales conversion rate from 20% to 24%.

3. Achievable:

- **Achievable Goal:** Increase revenue and improve the conversion rate within the company's capabilities and resources.

- **Assessment:** Based on market analysis and historical data, a 15% revenue increase and 20% conversion rate improvement are realistic targets for the company.

4. Relevant:

- **Relevant Goal:** Increasing revenue and improving the conversion rate directly contribute to the company's growth and profitability objectives.

- **Alignment:** These goals align with the company's strategic focus on expanding market share and enhancing sales performance in its target regions.

5. Time-bound:

- **Time-bound Goal:** Achieve the revenue and conversion rate targets within the next six months.

- **Timeline:** Goals are set for a specific timeframe of six months, providing a clear deadline for achievement.

Action Plan:

1. Marketing Campaigns: Launch targeted marketing campaigns to promote key products and drive customer engagement. Utilize email marketing, social media advertising, and promotional events to attract customers and generate sales leads.

2. Sales Training: Provide comprehensive training for sales staff to improve selling techniques, product knowledge, and customer service skills. Equip sales representatives with the tools and resources they need to effectively engage with customers and close sales.

3. Customer Relationship Management (CRM): Implement a CRM system to track customer interactions, manage leads, and monitor sales performance. Utilize CRM data to identify sales opportunities, prioritize leads, and streamline the sales process.

4. Sales Incentives: Introduce sales incentives and bonuses to motivate sales staff and reward high-performance. Offer bonuses for achieving sales targets, converting leads into customers, and exceeding revenue goals.

5. Customer Experience Enhancement: Enhance the customer experience both online and in-store to increase satisfaction and drive repeat business. Improve website navigation, optimize product listings, and provide personalized recommendations to enhance the shopping experience.

Monitoring and Evaluation:

1. Regular Reviews: Conduct monthly reviews to track progress towards sales goals and assess performance against targets. Evaluate sales revenue, conversion rates, and other key metrics to identify areas for improvement and adjust strategies as needed.

2. Performance Dashboards: Utilize performance dashboards and reports to visualize sales data and monitor key metrics in real-time. Analyze trends, identify patterns, and make data-driven decisions to optimize sales performance.

3. Feedback Mechanisms: Solicit feedback from sales staff, customers, and stakeholders to gain insights into sales performance and customer satisfaction. Use feedback to identify opportunities for improvement, address issues, and enhance the effectiveness of sales initiatives.

Conclusion:

By setting SMART goals and implementing a strategic action plan, XYZ Retail Inc. can drive sales performance, achieve revenue growth, and improve the conversion rate within the specified timeframe. Through effective monitoring, evaluation, and continuous improvement, the company can adapt to market dynamics, overcome challenges, and achieve its objectives of expanding market share and enhancing profitability.

CHAPTER III
Implementing Sales Analytics

3.1 Data Collection and Management

3.1.1 Identifying Relevant Data Sources

In the realm of sales analytics, the effectiveness of insights derived heavily relies on the quality and relevance of the data collected. Identifying the right data sources is foundational to this process. Businesses must strategically choose sources that provide comprehensive and accurate information to fuel their analytics efforts. This section delves into various data sources commonly utilized in sales analytics and the considerations associated with each.

Internal Data Sources:

1. CRM Systems: Customer Relationship Management (CRM) systems serve as a treasure trove of data for sales teams. They store information on leads, contacts, accounts, opportunities, and more. By extracting data from CRM platforms, organizations can gain insights into customer behavior, sales pipeline, conversion rates, and customer interactions. Additionally, CRM data can be integrated with other internal and external sources to enrich analysis.

2. Sales Transactions: Internal sales transaction data offers invaluable insights into revenue generation, product performance, and customer purchasing patterns. By analyzing transactional data, businesses can identify top-selling products, customer segments with high lifetime value, seasonal trends, and sales performance by region or salesperson. This data is typically captured in enterprise resource planning (ERP) systems or point-of-sale (POS) systems.

3. Marketing Automation Platforms: Marketing automation platforms track various marketing activities such as email campaigns, social media engagement, website traffic, and lead generation efforts. Integrating data from these platforms with sales analytics provides a holistic view of the customer journey, from initial touchpoints to conversion. Marketers can assess the effectiveness of different marketing channels and campaigns in driving sales and nurturing leads through the sales funnel.

External Data Sources:

1. Market Research Reports: External market research reports offer insights into industry trends, market dynamics, competitor analysis, and consumer behavior. These reports provide benchmarking data that helps businesses understand their market position and identify opportunities for growth. Leveraging third-party market research data enables organizations to make data-driven decisions and adapt their sales strategies to changing market conditions.

2. Social Media and Web Analytics: Social media platforms and website analytics tools capture vast amounts of data on user interactions, engagement metrics, and online behaviors. By analyzing social media mentions, likes, shares, and website traffic patterns, businesses can gauge brand awareness, customer sentiment, and the effectiveness of digital marketing efforts. Integrating social media and web analytics data with sales analytics provides a comprehensive view of the customer journey across online channels.

3. Industry Benchmarks and Databases: Industry-specific benchmarks and databases offer comparative data on key performance indicators (KPIs) such as sales growth, market share, and customer acquisition costs. Accessing industry benchmarks allows businesses to assess their performance relative to competitors and identify areas for improvement. These external benchmarks serve as reference points for setting sales targets, optimizing pricing strategies, and evaluating overall business performance.

Data Considerations:

1. Accuracy and Completeness: Ensuring the accuracy and completeness of data is paramount for meaningful analysis. Data quality issues such as duplicate records, missing values, and inconsistencies can compromise the integrity of analytics insights. Implementing data validation processes and data cleansing techniques helps maintain data quality standards and improve the reliability of analysis results.

2. Data Security and Privacy: Protecting sensitive customer data and ensuring compliance with data privacy regulations are critical considerations in data collection and management. Businesses must implement robust data security measures to safeguard confidential information and prevent unauthorized access or data breaches. Adhering to regulations such as the General Data Protection Regulation (GDPR) and the California Consumer Privacy Act (CCPA) is essential to maintaining customer trust and mitigating legal risks.

3. Data Governance and Compliance: Establishing clear data governance policies and procedures is essential for managing data effectively across the organization. Data governance frameworks define roles and responsibilities, data ownership, data access controls, and data lifecycle management practices. By promoting data governance best practices, businesses can enhance data integrity, foster collaboration, and ensure compliance with regulatory requirements.

In summary, identifying relevant data sources is a fundamental step in implementing sales analytics initiatives. By leveraging a combination of internal and external data sources, businesses can gain actionable insights into customer behavior, market trends, and sales performance. However, ensuring data accuracy, security, and compliance remains paramount to deriving meaningful and trustworthy analytics insights. By addressing these considerations, organizations can unlock the full potential of sales analytics to drive growth and profitability.

3.1.2 Data Quality Assurance

Data quality assurance is a critical aspect of any data-driven initiative, including sales analytics. Ensuring that the data used for analysis is accurate, reliable, and consistent is essential for generating meaningful insights and making informed business decisions. This section explores the importance of data quality assurance in sales analytics and outlines best practices for maintaining high-quality data.

Importance of Data Quality Assurance:

1. Enhanced Decision-Making: High-quality data serves as a reliable foundation for decision-making processes. By ensuring data accuracy and integrity, organizations can make informed decisions that drive business growth and performance. Inaccurate or inconsistent data can lead to flawed analysis and misguided strategies, resulting in missed opportunities and suboptimal outcomes.

2. Trust and Credibility: Data quality directly impacts the trust and credibility of analytics insights. Stakeholders, including executives, managers, and frontline sales teams, rely on analytics to guide their actions and strategies. Inconsistent or unreliable data erodes trust in the analytics process and undermines confidence in the resulting insights. By prioritizing data quality assurance, organizations can maintain trust in the accuracy and relevance of analytics outputs.

3. Cost Reduction: Poor data quality can result in significant costs for businesses, including wasted resources, ineffective marketing campaigns, and lost revenue opportunities. By proactively addressing data quality issues, organizations can minimize errors, improve operational efficiency, and optimize resource allocation. Investing in data quality assurance measures can ultimately lead to cost savings and improved return on investment (ROI) from sales analytics initiatives.

Best Practices for Data Quality Assurance:

1. Data Profiling: Data profiling involves analyzing data to assess its quality, completeness, and consistency. By profiling data sources, organizations can identify potential issues such as missing values, outliers, and data inconsistencies. Automated data profiling tools can streamline this process by providing insights into data quality metrics and highlighting areas that require attention.

2. Data Cleansing: Data cleansing, also known as data scrubbing or data cleaning, involves identifying and correcting errors or inconsistencies in the data. This process may include removing duplicate records, standardizing data formats, and validating data against predefined rules or constraints. Automated data cleansing tools can help streamline this process by identifying and resolving data quality issues efficiently.

3. Data Validation: Data validation ensures that data meets predefined quality criteria and business rules. This may involve performing validation checks to verify data accuracy, completeness, and consistency. Validation rules can be applied at various stages of the data lifecycle, including during data entry, data integration, and data transformation processes. Implementing robust data validation procedures helps maintain data quality standards and prevents the propagation of errors throughout the analytics pipeline.

4. Data Governance: Data governance encompasses the policies, processes, and controls that govern the management and use of data within an organization. Establishing a robust data governance framework is essential for maintaining data quality and integrity. This includes defining data ownership, roles, and responsibilities, establishing data quality standards, and implementing mechanisms for monitoring and enforcing compliance. By promoting a culture of data governance, organizations can ensure accountability and consistency in data management practices.

5. Continuous Monitoring: Data quality is not a one-time effort but requires ongoing monitoring and maintenance. Implementing regular data quality checks and audits helps identify emerging issues and ensures that data quality standards are upheld over time. Automated monitoring tools can alert stakeholders to potential data quality issues in real-time, enabling timely corrective action. By continuously monitoring data quality, organizations can proactively address issues before they escalate and maintain the reliability of analytics insights.

In conclusion, data quality assurance is essential for the success of sales analytics initiatives. By prioritizing data quality and implementing best practices for data collection, cleansing, validation, and governance, organizations can ensure that their analytics efforts yield accurate, reliable, and actionable insights. Investing in data quality assurance not only enhances decision-making and trust in analytics but also contributes to cost reduction and operational efficiency. By making data quality a priority, organizations can unlock the full potential of sales analytics to drive growth and competitiveness in today's dynamic business environment.

3.1.3 Data Integration

Data integration is a crucial component of sales analytics, facilitating the aggregation and consolidation of data from various sources to create a unified view of sales performance. By integrating disparate data sources, organizations can gain comprehensive insights into customer behavior, sales trends, and performance metrics. This section explores the importance of data integration in sales analytics and outlines best practices for implementing an effective data integration strategy.

Importance of Data Integration:

1. 360-Degree View of Customers: Data integration enables organizations to consolidate customer data from multiple sources, including CRM systems, marketing automation platforms, and transactional databases. By creating a unified view of customers, organizations can gain insights into customer preferences, purchase history, and interactions across different touchpoints. This 360-degree view of customers facilitates personalized sales and marketing strategies, improves customer segmentation, and enhances overall customer experience.

2. Holistic Sales Performance Analysis: Integrating data from various sales channels and systems provides a holistic view of sales performance across the organization. By combining data on sales transactions, lead generation activities, and pipeline metrics, organizations can analyze sales performance trends, identify revenue drivers, and assess the effectiveness of sales strategies. This comprehensive analysis enables sales leaders to make data-driven decisions and optimize sales processes for improved performance and growth.

3. Improved Forecasting and Predictive Analytics: Data integration lays the foundation for advanced analytics techniques such as forecasting and predictive modeling. By integrating historical sales data with external factors such as market trends, economic indicators, and seasonality, organizations can develop more accurate sales forecasts and predictive models. These insights help sales teams anticipate future demand, identify sales opportunities, and allocate resources more effectively to drive growth and profitability.

Best Practices for Data Integration:

1. Define Data Integration Objectives: Before embarking on a data integration initiative, organizations should clearly define their objectives and priorities. This includes identifying the types of data to be integrated, the sources of data, and the desired outcomes. Establishing clear objectives helps align data integration efforts with business goals and ensures that the integration process addresses specific business needs and challenges.

2. Choose the Right Integration Approach: There are various approaches to data integration, including ETL (extract, transform, load), ELT (extract, load, transform), data virtualization, and API-based integration. Organizations should evaluate the pros and cons of each approach based on factors such as data volume, complexity, latency requirements, and scalability. Selecting the right integration approach ensures efficient data movement and transformation while minimizing disruptions to existing systems and processes.

3. Standardize Data Formats and Definitions: Standardizing data formats, naming conventions, and definitions is essential for ensuring consistency and interoperability across integrated data sources. Establishing data standards simplifies the integration process, reduces data errors, and facilitates data governance and metadata management. Organizations should develop data governance policies and data dictionaries to document data standards and promote adherence across the organization.

4. Implement Data Quality Checks: Data quality assurance is a critical aspect of data integration. Organizations should implement data quality checks and validation rules to ensure the accuracy, completeness, and consistency of integrated data. This may involve performing data profiling, cleansing, and deduplication processes to identify and resolve data quality issues before they affect analytics insights. Automated data quality tools can streamline these processes and provide real-time feedback on data quality metrics.

5. Establish Data Governance and Security Measures: Data governance and security are paramount considerations in data integration efforts. Organizations should establish robust data governance frameworks to define roles, responsibilities, and processes for managing integrated data. This includes implementing access controls, encryption, and data masking techniques to protect sensitive information and ensure compliance with data privacy regulations. Regular audits and monitoring mechanisms help maintain data integrity and mitigate security risks associated with integrated data.

6. Enable Real-Time Integration and Automation: In today's fast-paced business environment, real-time data integration is increasingly important for timely decision-making and responsiveness. Organizations should leverage technologies such as event-driven architecture, streaming data processing, and cloud-based integration platforms to enable real-time data integration and automation. By automating data integration processes, organizations can reduce manual effort, improve data freshness, and accelerate time-to-insight.

In conclusion, data integration is a critical enabler of sales analytics, providing organizations with a unified view of sales performance and customer insights. By integrating data from disparate sources and applying best practices for data integration, organizations can unlock the full potential of sales analytics to drive growth, improve decision-making, and enhance customer relationships. Investing in data integration capabilities ensures that organizations have access to timely, accurate, and actionable data to support their sales initiatives and achieve their business objectives.

3.2 Tools and Technologies for Sales Analytics

Sales analytics relies heavily on various tools and technologies to collect, process, analyze, and visualize data effectively. These tools play a crucial role in empowering sales teams to make data-driven decisions, optimize sales strategies, and drive business growth. This section explores one of the fundamental tools for sales analytics: CRM systems.

3.2.1 CRM Systems

Customer Relationship Management (CRM) systems are central to sales analytics, serving as a foundational tool for managing customer interactions, tracking sales activities, and analyzing customer data. CRM systems provide a comprehensive platform for storing and accessing valuable customer information, enabling sales teams to streamline processes, enhance customer relationships, and drive sales performance.

Key Features of CRM Systems:

1. Contact Management: CRM systems serve as centralized repositories for storing customer contact information, including names, addresses, phone numbers, and email addresses. Sales teams can easily access and update contact records, enabling efficient communication and relationship management.

2. Sales Pipeline Management: CRM systems facilitate the tracking and management of sales opportunities through various stages of the sales pipeline. Sales teams can monitor the progress of deals, assign tasks, and set reminders for follow-up activities, ensuring timely engagement and effective pipeline management.

3. Activity Tracking: CRM systems capture and log various sales activities, including calls, emails, meetings, and interactions with prospects and customers. This allows sales representatives to track their activities, prioritize tasks, and maintain a record of customer interactions for future reference.

4. Lead Management: CRM systems enable organizations to capture and qualify leads effectively, ensuring that sales teams focus their efforts on high-potential opportunities. Leads can be assigned scores or rankings based on predefined criteria, allowing sales teams to prioritize follow-up activities and allocate resources efficiently.

5. Reporting and Analytics: CRM systems offer robust reporting and analytics capabilities, allowing organizations to derive insights from sales data and track key performance metrics. Sales managers can generate reports on sales performance, pipeline health, conversion rates, and other critical indicators to assess team performance and identify areas for improvement.

6. Integration with Other Systems: Modern CRM systems offer integration capabilities with other business systems and tools, such as marketing automation platforms, ERP systems, and BI tools. This seamless integration enables organizations to exchange data between different systems, eliminate silos, and create a unified view of customer interactions and business operations.

Benefits of CRM Systems for Sales Analytics:

1. Improved Sales Efficiency: CRM systems streamline sales processes, automate repetitive tasks, and provide sales teams with the tools they need to work more efficiently. By centralizing customer data and sales activities, CRM systems eliminate manual data entry and administrative overhead, allowing sales representatives to focus on selling and building relationships.

2. Enhanced Customer Relationships: CRM systems enable organizations to better understand their customers' needs, preferences, and behaviors. By capturing and analyzing customer data, organizations can personalize interactions, anticipate needs, and deliver tailored solutions that drive customer satisfaction and loyalty.

3. Data-Driven Decision Making: CRM systems provide sales managers and executives with real-time insights into sales performance and customer trends. By leveraging CRM analytics, organizations can identify sales opportunities, forecast future revenue, and make data-driven decisions that drive business growth.

4. Scalability and Flexibility: CRM systems are highly scalable and adaptable, allowing organizations to accommodate growth and change over time. Whether expanding into new markets, adding new products or services, or scaling sales operations, CRM systems can support evolving business needs and processes.

Best Practices for Implementing CRM Systems:

1. Define Clear Objectives: Before implementing a CRM system, organizations should define clear objectives and requirements based on their business goals and sales processes. This includes identifying key features, integration needs, user roles, and success metrics to ensure that the CRM system aligns with business objectives.

2. User Adoption and Training: User adoption is critical to the success of a CRM implementation. Organizations should provide comprehensive training and support to ensure that users understand how to use the CRM system effectively. This may include hands-on training sessions, user manuals, online tutorials, and ongoing support resources.

3. Customization and Configuration: CRM systems should be customized and configured to meet the specific needs of the organization and its sales teams. This may involve customizing fields, workflows, and reports to align with sales processes and data requirements. Organizations should also ensure that the CRM system integrates seamlessly with existing systems and tools to maximize efficiency and data accuracy.

4. Data Quality and Governance: Maintaining data quality is essential for the effectiveness of a CRM system. Organizations should establish data governance policies and procedures to ensure data accuracy, completeness, and consistency. This includes implementing data validation rules, de-duplication processes, and regular data hygiene practices to keep CRM data clean and reliable.

5. Continuous Improvement and Optimization: CRM implementations should be viewed as ongoing initiatives that require continuous improvement and optimization. Organizations should regularly review and assess CRM usage, performance metrics, and user feedback to identify areas for improvement and optimization. This may involve fine-tuning workflows, updating configurations, and incorporating new features or integrations to enhance the CRM system's effectiveness over time.

In conclusion, CRM systems are indispensable tools for sales analytics, providing organizations with the capabilities to manage customer relationships, track sales activities, and derive insights from sales data. By leveraging CRM systems effectively and implementing best practices for CRM implementation and usage, organizations can optimize sales processes, enhance customer relationships, and drive business growth and profitability. Investing in a robust CRM system is essential for organizations looking to harness the power of sales analytics and stay competitive in today's dynamic business landscape.

3.2.2 Business Intelligence (BI) Tools

Business Intelligence (BI) tools are essential components of the sales analytics toolkit, providing capabilities for data analysis, reporting, and decision support. These tools empower organizations to extract actionable insights from their data, identify trends, and optimize sales strategies. In this section, we will explore the role of BI tools in sales analytics and discuss key features and considerations for selecting and implementing BI solutions.

Role of Business Intelligence (BI) Tools in Sales Analytics:

1. Data Integration and Transformation: BI tools enable organizations to integrate data from multiple sources, including CRM systems, ERP systems, spreadsheets, and external databases. These tools provide capabilities for data cleansing, transformation, and enrichment, ensuring that data is accurate, consistent, and ready for analysis.

2. Data Analysis and Exploration: BI tools offer a wide range of analytical capabilities, including ad-hoc querying, OLAP (Online Analytical Processing), and data visualization. Sales teams can analyze sales performance, customer behavior, and market trends using intuitive interfaces and interactive dashboards. Advanced analytics features such as predictive modeling, forecasting, and what-if analysis enable organizations to anticipate future outcomes and make proactive decisions.

3. Reporting and Dashboards: BI tools enable organizations to create customized reports, dashboards, and scorecards to track key performance indicators (KPIs) and monitor sales performance in real-time. These reports can be scheduled, automated, and distributed to stakeholders across the organization, ensuring that decision-makers have access to timely and actionable insights.

4. Data Governance and Security: BI tools provide capabilities for data governance, access control, and security, ensuring that sensitive information is protected and compliance requirements are met. Organizations can define role-based access controls, encryption policies, and auditing mechanisms to safeguard data privacy and integrity.

5. Collaboration and Sharing: BI tools facilitate collaboration and knowledge sharing among sales teams, enabling users to annotate, comment, and share insights within the platform. Collaborative features such as discussion threads, shared workspaces, and version control ensure that insights are communicated effectively and decision-making processes are transparent.

Key Features and Considerations for Selecting BI Tools:

1. Ease of Use and Accessibility: Choose BI tools that offer intuitive interfaces and user-friendly features, allowing sales teams to analyze data and create reports without extensive technical expertise. Look for tools that support self-service analytics and empower users to explore data independently.

2. Scalability and Performance: Evaluate the scalability and performance of BI tools to ensure that they can handle large volumes of data and support growing user demands. Consider factors such as data processing speed, concurrency, and support for distributed architectures.

3. Integration Capabilities: Select BI tools that integrate seamlessly with existing systems and data sources, including CRM systems, data warehouses, and cloud platforms. Ensure that the BI tool supports common data formats and protocols for data ingestion, transformation, and interoperability.

4. Advanced Analytics Capabilities: Assess the advanced analytics capabilities of BI tools, including predictive modeling, machine learning, and natural language processing. These capabilities enable organizations to uncover hidden insights, automate repetitive tasks, and drive innovation in sales analytics.

5. Flexibility and Customization: Look for BI tools that offer flexibility and customization options to adapt to the unique needs and requirements of the organization. Consider the ability to create custom reports, dashboards, and data visualizations tailored to specific use cases and user preferences.

6. Support and Training: Evaluate the level of support, training, and documentation provided by BI tool vendors to ensure that users can maximize the value of the tool. Look for vendors that offer comprehensive training programs, online resources, and dedicated support channels to assist users with onboarding and troubleshooting.

7. Cost and Licensing: Consider the cost structure and licensing model of BI tools, including upfront costs, ongoing maintenance fees, and scalability options. Compare pricing plans from different vendors and evaluate the total cost of ownership over the lifetime of the tool.

In conclusion, Business Intelligence (BI) tools play a critical role in enabling organizations to harness the power of sales analytics and drive informed decision-making. By providing capabilities for data integration, analysis, reporting, and collaboration, BI tools empower sales teams to extract actionable insights from their data and optimize sales performance. When selecting BI tools, consider key features such as ease of use, scalability, integration capabilities, advanced analytics, flexibility, support, and cost to ensure that the chosen solution meets the organization's needs and objectives. Investing in BI tools is essential for organizations looking to gain a competitive edge in today's data-driven business landscape and achieve sustainable growth and success.

3.2.3 Predictive Analytics Platforms

Predictive analytics platforms are instrumental in leveraging historical data to forecast future outcomes and trends in sales. These platforms utilize advanced statistical algorithms, machine learning techniques, and data mining capabilities to identify patterns, make predictions, and inform strategic decision-making. In this section, we will delve into the role of predictive analytics platforms in sales analytics, discuss key features, and explore considerations for selecting and implementing these platforms.

Role of Predictive Analytics Platforms in Sales Analytics:

1. Forecasting Sales Performance: Predictive analytics platforms analyze historical sales data, customer demographics, market trends, and other relevant variables to forecast future sales performance. By identifying patterns and correlations in the data, these platforms enable organizations to anticipate demand, identify growth opportunities, and optimize sales strategies.

2. Customer Segmentation and Targeting: Predictive analytics platforms segment customers based on their characteristics, behavior, and purchasing patterns. By clustering similar customers into distinct segments, organizations can tailor marketing campaigns, promotions, and sales strategies to target specific customer segments effectively. This personalized approach improves customer engagement, loyalty, and conversion rates.

3. Lead Scoring and Prioritization: Predictive analytics platforms assess the likelihood of leads converting into customers based on various factors such as demographic information, past interactions, and engagement levels. By assigning scores or rankings to leads, organizations can prioritize sales efforts, allocate resources effectively, and focus on high-potential opportunities that are most likely to result in conversions.

4. Churn Prediction and Customer Retention: Predictive analytics platforms analyze customer behavior, satisfaction levels, and engagement metrics to predict the likelihood of churn or customer attrition. By identifying at-risk customers early on, organizations can implement proactive retention strategies, such as targeted promotions, loyalty programs, and personalized interventions, to prevent churn and maximize customer lifetime value.

5. Inventory Optimization: Predictive analytics platforms forecast product demand and inventory requirements based on historical sales data, market trends, and seasonality. By accurately predicting demand fluctuations and stockouts, organizations can optimize inventory levels, minimize excess inventory costs, and ensure timely replenishment to meet customer demand.

Key Features and Considerations for Selecting Predictive Analytics Platforms:

1. Algorithmic Capabilities: Evaluate the algorithmic capabilities of predictive analytics platforms, including regression analysis, decision trees, neural networks, and ensemble methods. Consider the scalability, accuracy, and interpretability of the algorithms, as well as their suitability for different types of predictive modeling tasks.

2. Data Integration and Preparation: Assess the platform's capabilities for integrating and preparing data from disparate sources, including CRM systems, ERP systems, transactional databases, and external data sources. Look for features such as data cleansing, normalization, and feature engineering to ensure that data is clean, structured, and ready for analysis.

3. Model Building and Deployment: Consider the platform's tools and workflows for building, training, and deploying predictive models. Look for features such as automated model selection, hyperparameter tuning, and model validation to streamline the model development process and ensure optimal performance. Evaluate the platform's deployment options, including on-premises, cloud-based, and hybrid deployments, to choose the deployment model that best fits your organization's needs and infrastructure.

4. Scalability and Performance: Assess the platform's scalability and performance capabilities to handle large volumes of data and support growing user demands. Consider factors such as processing speed, memory usage, and support for distributed computing to ensure that the platform can handle the scalability requirements of your organization.

5. Interpretability and Explainability: Evaluate the platform's ability to provide insights into the underlying factors driving predictions and recommendations. Look for features such as model interpretability, variable importance analysis, and decision explanations to understand how predictive models arrive at their conclusions and make informed decisions based on the insights generated.

6. Integration with Existing Systems: Ensure that the predictive analytics platform integrates seamlessly with existing systems and tools within your organization's IT ecosystem. Evaluate compatibility with common data formats, APIs, and integration protocols to facilitate data exchange and interoperability with other systems, such as CRM systems, BI tools, and data warehouses.

7. Support and Training: Consider the level of support, training, and documentation provided by the predictive analytics platform vendor. Look for vendors that offer comprehensive training programs, user guides, online resources, and dedicated support channels to assist users with onboarding, troubleshooting, and maximizing the value of the platform.

8. Regulatory Compliance and Security: Assess the platform's compliance with regulatory requirements such as GDPR, HIPAA, and CCPA, as well as industry-specific standards and regulations. Ensure that the platform provides robust security features, including data encryption, access controls, and audit trails, to protect sensitive information and ensure data privacy and integrity.

In conclusion, predictive analytics platforms play a pivotal role in driving sales analytics by leveraging historical data to forecast future outcomes and trends. By harnessing advanced statistical algorithms, machine learning techniques, and data mining capabilities, these platforms enable organizations to make data-driven decisions, optimize sales strategies, and maximize business performance. When selecting predictive analytics platforms, consider key features such as algorithmic capabilities, data integration and preparation, model building and deployment, scalability and performance, interpretability and explainability, integration with existing systems, support and training, and regulatory compliance and security to ensure that the chosen platform meets the organization's needs and objectives. Investing in predictive analytics platforms is essential for organizations looking to gain a competitive edge, mitigate risks, and capitalize on opportunities in today's dynamic and data-driven business landscape.

3.3 Data Visualization Techniques

Data visualization is a powerful tool in sales analytics, enabling organizations to communicate complex information in a clear and visually compelling manner. Dashboards, in particular, serve as the interface through which users interact with data and gain insights into sales performance. This section explores the principles of dashboard design and best practices for creating effective sales analytics dashboards.

3.3.1 Dashboard Design Principles

Effective dashboard design is essential for delivering actionable insights and facilitating informed decision-making. Dashboards should be intuitive, visually appealing, and designed with the end user in mind. The following principles guide the design and development of successful sales analytics dashboards:

1. Understand User Needs:

   - Before designing a dashboard, it's essential to understand the needs and preferences of the end users. Identify the key stakeholders who will be using the dashboard and gather insights into their goals, workflows, and information requirements. Tailor the dashboard design to address the specific needs of different user groups, such as sales managers, executives, and frontline sales representatives.

2. Define Clear Objectives:

   - Clearly define the objectives and purpose of the dashboard to ensure that it aligns with business goals and user expectations. Determine the primary questions the dashboard should answer and the key performance indicators (KPIs) it should track. Establishing clear objectives helps focus the design process and ensures that the dashboard provides actionable insights that drive business outcomes.

3. Keep it Simple and Focused:

- Avoid clutter and unnecessary complexity in dashboard design. Keep the layout clean and organized, with a focus on presenting the most relevant information prominently. Use concise labels, meaningful visuals, and intuitive navigation to guide users' attention to critical insights. Limit the number of charts, graphs, and data points to avoid overwhelming users and maintain clarity.

4. Choose Appropriate Visualizations:

- Select visualizations that effectively communicate the underlying data and support users' understanding of key insights. Choose chart types that best represent the data relationships and trends, such as bar charts, line graphs, pie charts, and heatmaps. Consider the audience's familiarity with different visualization formats and their preferences for interpreting data.

5. Maintain Consistency and Cohesion:

- Maintain consistency in design elements, such as color schemes, fonts, and layout, to create a cohesive visual experience across the dashboard. Use color strategically to highlight important information, indicate trends, and differentiate data categories. Ensure that labels, legends, and annotations are consistently applied throughout the dashboard to aid interpretation and reduce confusion.

6. Provide Interactivity and Drill-Down Capabilities:

- Enhance user engagement and exploration by incorporating interactive features and drill-down capabilities into the dashboard. Allow users to filter data, adjust time periods, and explore different dimensions of the data dynamically. Interactive elements such as clickable buttons, dropdown menus, and sliders enable users to customize their view and focus on specific areas of interest.

7. Prioritize Accessibility and Usability:

- Design dashboards with accessibility and usability in mind to ensure that all users can effectively interact with the data. Consider factors such as color contrast, text legibility, and screen reader compatibility to accommodate users with disabilities. Optimize the dashboard for various devices and screen sizes to provide a seamless user experience across desktops, tablets, and mobile devices.

8. Iterate and Iterate:

- Dashboard design is an iterative process that requires continuous refinement based on user feedback and evolving business needs. Gather input from stakeholders and end users throughout the design and development process to identify areas for improvement and optimization. Iterate on the design based on user testing, usability studies, and performance metrics to create a dashboard that meets users' needs effectively.

In conclusion, effective dashboard design is essential for maximizing the value of sales analytics and empowering users to make data-driven decisions. By adhering to these principles and best practices, organizations can create intuitive, visually appealing dashboards that deliver actionable insights, drive business performance, and facilitate collaboration across sales teams. Investing in thoughtful dashboard design not only enhances user engagement and productivity but also ensures that sales analytics efforts contribute to the organization's overall growth and success.

3.3.2 Visualization Best Practices

Data visualization is a powerful tool for conveying complex information in a clear and concise manner. Effective visualization techniques enhance understanding, facilitate decision-making, and uncover insights hidden within data. In the context of sales analytics, choosing the right visualization methods is crucial for effectively communicating sales performance, trends, and patterns. This section outlines best practices for selecting and creating visualizations in sales analytics.

1. Understand Your Audience:

- Before creating visualizations, it's essential to understand the audience who will be consuming them. Consider their level of expertise in data analysis, their familiarity with visualization techniques, and their specific information needs. Tailor visualizations to the audience's preferences and knowledge level to ensure maximum effectiveness.

2. Choose the Right Visualization Type:

- Different types of data call for different visualization techniques. Select the visualization type that best represents the data relationships and patterns. Common visualization types used in sales analytics include:

   - Bar charts: Suitable for comparing discrete categories or showing trends over time.

   - Line charts: Ideal for displaying trends or changes in data over time.

   - Pie charts: Useful for illustrating proportions or percentages of a whole.

   - Scatter plots: Effective for showing relationships between two variables.

   - Heatmaps: Helpful for visualizing patterns or densities in large datasets.

   - Geospatial maps: Great for displaying sales data by geographic location.

3. Keep it Simple:

- Avoid clutter and unnecessary complexity in visualizations. Simplify the design by focusing on the most critical information and removing unnecessary elements. Use clear labels, concise titles, and intuitive color schemes to enhance readability and comprehension. Remember, simplicity leads to clarity.

4. Use Color Wisely:

- Color can enhance visual appeal and convey meaning in visualizations, but it should be used judiciously. Choose a color palette that is visually pleasing and accessible to all users, including those with color vision deficiencies. Use color strategically to highlight key data points, trends, or categories, but avoid using too many colors, which can cause confusion.

5. Provide Context:

- Context is essential for interpreting visualizations accurately. Provide clear titles, axis labels, and legends to help users understand the data and its significance. Include annotations or explanatory text where necessary to provide additional context or insights. Consider incorporating reference lines or benchmarks to highlight targets or thresholds.

6. Ensure Interactivity:

- Interactive visualizations enable users to explore data dynamically and gain deeper insights. Incorporate interactive features such as tooltips, filters, and drill-down capabilities to enhance user engagement and exploration. Allow users to interact with the data by selecting specific data points, adjusting parameters, or filtering results based on criteria of interest.

7. Maintain Consistency:

- Consistency in visualization design promotes coherence and ease of understanding. Use consistent formatting, labeling conventions, and visualization styles across all visualizations within a dashboard or report. This consistency helps users navigate the information seamlessly and reduces cognitive load.

8. Test and Iterate:

- Testing is essential to ensure that visualizations effectively convey the intended message and resonate with the audience. Conduct user testing and gather feedback to identify areas for improvement and optimization. Iterate on the design based on user input and insights gained from testing to create visualizations that meet users' needs and expectations.

9. Consider Accessibility:

- Accessibility is a crucial consideration in visualization design to ensure that all users can access and interpret the information effectively. Use accessible colors, provide alternative text for images, and ensure that visualizations are compatible with screen readers and other assistive technologies. Design visualizations with a focus on inclusivity to accommodate users with diverse needs and abilities.

10. Stay Updated on Visualization Trends:

   - The field of data visualization is continuously evolving, with new techniques and trends emerging regularly. Stay updated on the latest developments in visualization design and incorporate innovative approaches into your visualizations where appropriate. Experiment with new tools, technologies, and visualization libraries to push the boundaries of what's possible and create engaging, impactful visualizations.

In summary, visualization best practices play a critical role in maximizing the effectiveness of sales analytics. By understanding the audience, choosing the right visualization types, keeping visualizations simple yet informative, providing context, ensuring interactivity and consistency, testing and iterating on designs, considering accessibility, and staying updated on visualization trends, organizations can create visualizations that deliver meaningful insights and drive informed decision-making in sales. Investing in effective visualization techniques is key to unlocking the full potential of sales analytics and achieving business growth and success.

3.3.3 Interpretation of Visual Data

Interpreting visual data is a crucial skill in sales analytics, as it allows stakeholders to derive meaningful insights and make informed decisions based on the information presented in visualizations. Effective interpretation involves understanding the context of the data, identifying trends and patterns, and drawing actionable conclusions. This section outlines best practices for interpreting visual data in sales analytics.

1. Understand the Context:

   - Before interpreting visual data, it's essential to understand the context in which the data was collected and the purpose of the visualization. Consider the objectives of the analysis, the target audience, and any relevant background information or business insights. Understanding the context helps ensure that interpretations are relevant and actionable.

2. Focus on Key Metrics:

- Identify the key metrics or performance indicators depicted in the visualization and focus your interpretation on these metrics. Look for trends, patterns, or anomalies that provide insights into sales performance, customer behavior, or market dynamics. Pay attention to changes over time, comparisons between different segments or regions, and deviations from expected norms.

3. Look for Patterns and Trends:

- Visual data often reveals patterns and trends that may not be apparent from raw data alone. Look for trends such as upward or downward trajectories, seasonality, or cyclicality in the data. Identify patterns such as correlations, clusters, or outliers that may indicate underlying relationships or anomalies. Understanding these patterns and trends can help uncover opportunities or risks in sales performance.

4. Compare and Contrast:

- Compare visualizations across different time periods, geographic regions, product categories, or customer segments to identify variations and trends. Look for differences or similarities in performance metrics and analyze the factors contributing to these differences. Contrasting visualizations can provide valuable insights into sales dynamics and help prioritize areas for improvement or investment.

5. Consider the Data Granularity:

- Pay attention to the granularity of the data presented in visualizations and consider its implications for interpretation. Aggregated data may provide a high-level overview of sales performance, while disaggregated data may reveal more detailed insights into individual transactions or customer interactions. Adjust the level of granularity as needed to gain a comprehensive understanding of sales trends and patterns.

6. Contextualize with External Factors:

- Consider external factors that may influence sales performance and interpret visual data in the context of these factors. External factors may include market conditions, economic trends, competitive landscape, marketing campaigns, or seasonality. Analyze how these factors impact sales metrics and adjust interpretations accordingly.

7. Validate Insights with Additional Data:

- Validate insights derived from visual data by comparing them with additional data sources or conducting further analysis. Look for corroborating evidence or alternative explanations for observed patterns or trends. Use statistical techniques, hypothesis testing, or predictive modeling to assess the robustness of insights and refine interpretations as needed.

8. Communicate Insights Effectively:

- Communicate insights derived from visual data effectively to stakeholders using clear and concise language. Highlight key findings, implications, and recommendations based on the analysis. Use visual cues such as annotations, callouts, or highlights to draw attention to important insights within the visualization. Tailor the communication to the audience's level of expertise and familiarity with the data.

9. Iterate and Refine Interpretations:

- Interpretation of visual data is an iterative process that requires ongoing refinement and validation. Continuously review and refine interpretations based on new data, feedback from stakeholders, and changing business requirements. Iterate on the analysis to uncover deeper insights, refine hypotheses, and adapt strategies based on evolving insights.

10. Foster Collaboration and Discussion:

- Encourage collaboration and discussion among stakeholders when interpreting visual data. Foster an environment where diverse perspectives and expertise can contribute to richer insights and decision-making. Engage stakeholders in discussions around the implications of visual data, potential action plans, and next steps to drive alignment and consensus.

In summary, effective interpretation of visual data is essential for unlocking the value of sales analytics and driving informed decision-making. By understanding the context, focusing on key metrics, identifying patterns and trends, comparing and contrasting data, considering external factors, validating insights, communicating effectively, iterating and refining interpretations, and fostering collaboration, organizations can derive actionable insights from visual data that drive business growth and performance. Investing in interpretation skills and best practices empowers stakeholders to harness the full potential of visual data in sales analytics and achieve strategic objectives.

CHAPTER IV
Sales Forecasting Techniques

4.1 Historical Data Analysis

Historical data analysis is a foundational component of sales forecasting, providing insights into past trends, patterns, and behaviors that can inform future predictions. By analyzing historical sales data, organizations can identify key drivers of sales performance, understand seasonality and trends, and develop accurate forecasts to guide strategic decision-making. In this section, we will explore the technique of time series analysis within the realm of historical data analysis, its methodologies, and its applications in sales forecasting.

4.1.1 Time Series Analysis

Time series analysis is a statistical method used to analyze sequential data points collected over regular intervals of time. In the context of sales forecasting, time series analysis involves examining historical sales data to identify patterns, trends, and seasonal fluctuations over time. By understanding the underlying patterns in the data, organizations can make informed predictions about future sales performance and adjust their strategies accordingly.

Methodologies of Time Series Analysis:

1. Descriptive Analysis: The first step in time series analysis involves descriptive statistics to summarize the historical sales data. This includes measures such as mean, median, standard deviation, and variance to understand the central tendency, variability, and distribution of sales over time.

2. Visualization Techniques: Visualizing the time series data using line charts, bar graphs, or heatmaps can provide insights into trends, seasonality, and anomalies. Trend lines, moving averages, and seasonal decomposition plots can help identify underlying patterns and fluctuations in the data.

3. Decomposition Methods: Decomposition methods such as additive or multiplicative decomposition can separate the time series data into its components: trend, seasonality, and random noise. This decomposition allows organizations to analyze each component separately and understand their individual contributions to sales performance.

4. Smoothing Techniques: Smoothing techniques such as exponential smoothing or moving averages can help remove noise and fluctuations from the time series data, making underlying patterns more visible. These techniques can provide a clearer picture of the underlying trends and facilitate more accurate forecasts.

5. Autocorrelation Analysis: Autocorrelation analysis examines the relationship between observations at different time lags. Autocorrelation plots and autocorrelation function (ACF) plots can help identify significant lagged relationships and determine the appropriate lag order for time series models.

6. Time Series Models: Time series models such as ARIMA (AutoRegressive Integrated Moving Average), SARIMA (Seasonal ARIMA), or exponential smoothing models can be used to forecast future sales based on historical patterns. These models incorporate trend, seasonality, and autocorrelation components to generate forecasts with varying degrees of complexity and accuracy.

Applications of Time Series Analysis in Sales Forecasting:

1. Demand Forecasting: Time series analysis enables organizations to forecast future demand for products or services based on historical sales data. By identifying trends, seasonality, and other patterns in the data, organizations can anticipate fluctuations in demand and adjust production, inventory, and supply chain management accordingly.

2. Sales Planning: Time series analysis informs sales planning and resource allocation decisions by providing insights into expected sales volumes, revenue projections, and growth trajectories. By forecasting future sales performance, organizations can set realistic targets, allocate resources effectively, and optimize sales strategies to achieve business objectives.

3. Inventory Management: Time series analysis helps organizations optimize inventory levels by forecasting future demand and adjusting inventory levels accordingly. By aligning inventory levels with anticipated sales volumes, organizations can minimize stockouts, reduce carrying costs, and improve overall inventory efficiency.

4. Marketing Campaign Planning: Time series analysis guides marketing campaign planning by identifying peak sales periods, seasonal trends, and other factors influencing consumer behavior. By aligning marketing activities with anticipated demand patterns, organizations can maximize the effectiveness of marketing campaigns, drive sales growth, and enhance customer engagement.

5. Financial Planning and Budgeting: Time series analysis supports financial planning and budgeting processes by providing insights into expected revenue streams, cash flows, and financial performance over time. By forecasting future sales, organizations can develop accurate financial projections, allocate budgets effectively, and make strategic investment decisions to drive growth and profitability.

In conclusion, time series analysis is a powerful technique for analyzing historical sales data and forecasting future sales performance. By examining trends, seasonality, and patterns in the data, organizations can make informed predictions about future sales volumes, revenue, and demand, guiding strategic decision-making and driving business growth. By leveraging the methodologies and applications of time series analysis outlined in this section, organizations can develop accurate sales forecasts, optimize resource allocation, and achieve their sales targets and objectives.

More detailed and specific examples for each methodology of time series analysis applied to the sales data of our retail company:

1. Descriptive Analysis:

- **Example:** The retail company collects monthly sales data for the past five years, including total sales revenue, number of transactions, and average transaction value.

- **Application:** Descriptive statistics are computed for each variable, such as mean, median, standard deviation, and variance. For instance, the mean monthly sales revenue is calculated to be $100,000, with a standard deviation of $10,000, indicating the variability in sales performance over time. These statistics provide a summary of the central tendency, variability, and distribution of sales data, aiding in understanding its characteristics.

2. Visualization Techniques:

- **Example:** Line charts are utilized to visualize monthly sales revenue over the past five years. The chart displays trends, seasonality, and fluctuations in sales performance over time, highlighting peak periods and low seasons.

- **Application:** By visually examining the sales data, the company can identify patterns, trends, and seasonality. For instance, if the line chart shows an upward trend in sales revenue over time with consistent peaks during the holiday season, the company can infer the impact of seasonality on sales performance and plan accordingly.

3. Decomposition Methods:

- **Example:** The sales data is decomposed into trend, seasonality, and random noise components using additive decomposition.

- **Application:** Additive decomposition separates the sales data into its constituent components, allowing the company to analyze each component separately. For instance, if the trend component shows a steady increase in sales over time, while the seasonal component exhibits recurring patterns in sales during specific months, the company can better understand the drivers of sales performance and make more accurate forecasts.

4. Smoothing Techniques:

- **Example:** Exponential smoothing techniques are applied to smooth out short-term fluctuations in the sales data.

- **Application:** Exponential smoothing removes noise and short-term variability from the sales data, making underlying trends more visible. For example, if the sales data exhibits random fluctuations or spikes due to temporary factors, exponential smoothing can help identify the underlying trend more accurately, aiding in forecasting future sales performance with greater precision.

5. Autocorrelation Analysis:

- **Example:** Autocorrelation plots are used to examine the relationship between sales data at different time lags.

- **Application:** Autocorrelation plots help identify significant correlations between observations at different time lags. For instance, if the autocorrelation plot shows high autocorrelation at lag 12 (indicating a yearly pattern), the company can infer the presence of seasonality in the sales data and adjust its forecasting models accordingly, considering the seasonal effects.

6. Time Series Models:

- **Example:** The company applies ARIMA models to forecast future sales revenue based on historical patterns, trend, and seasonality.

- **Application:** ARIMA models incorporate autoregression, differencing, and moving average components to capture the underlying patterns in the sales data and generate accurate forecasts. For example, if the ARIMA model predicts an increase in sales revenue during the holiday season based on historical trends and seasonality, the company can adjust its inventory levels, marketing strategies, and resource allocation to capitalize on the anticipated surge in sales.

In summary, by applying detailed methodologies of time series analysis such as descriptive analysis, visualization techniques, decomposition methods, smoothing techniques, autocorrelation analysis, and time series models to its sales data, the retail company can gain deep insights into sales performance, identify patterns and trends, and make informed decisions to drive growth and profitability effectively.

4.1.2 Trend Analysis

Trend analysis is a fundamental aspect of historical data analysis within sales forecasting. It involves identifying and analyzing patterns or trends in historical sales data to make informed predictions about future sales performance. By understanding historical trends, businesses can adapt their strategies and make more accurate forecasts to drive growth and optimize resources effectively.

Understanding Trends

Trends in sales data refer to the general direction in which sales are moving over time. These trends can be upward, indicating growth, downward, suggesting decline, or relatively stable. Trend analysis involves examining sales data over a specific period, identifying patterns, and extrapolating those patterns to make predictions about future performance.

Techniques for Trend Analysis

Several techniques can be employed for trend analysis:

1. Simple Moving Averages (SMA): SMA calculates the average of a specific number of data points over a defined period. This technique smoothens out fluctuations in data and highlights underlying trends. By adjusting the number of periods considered, analysts can capture short-term or long-term trends.

2. Exponential Smoothing: Exponential smoothing assigns exponentially decreasing weights to past observations. It gives more weight to recent data points while still considering older observations. This technique is particularly useful for detecting trends in noisy data or when there are sudden changes in sales patterns.

3. Linear Regression: Linear regression is a statistical method used to model the relationship between a dependent variable (sales) and one or more independent variables (time). It calculates a line that best fits the historical data points, allowing analysts to identify the direction and strength of the trend.

4. Seasonal Decomposition: Seasonal decomposition separates the time series data into trend, seasonal, and residual components. By isolating the trend component, analysts can gain a clearer understanding of the underlying long-term growth or decline in sales.

Interpretation of Trend Analysis Results

Interpreting the results of trend analysis requires careful consideration of various factors:

1. Direction: Determine whether the trend is upward, downward, or flat. An upward trend indicates growth, a downward trend signals decline, while a flat trend suggests stability.

2. Magnitude: Assess the steepness or slope of the trend line to gauge the rate of change in sales. A steeper slope indicates rapid growth or decline, while a gentle slope suggests gradual changes.

3. Consistency: Evaluate the consistency of the trend over time. A consistent trend strengthens the reliability of forecasts, whereas erratic fluctuations may require further analysis to identify underlying causes.

4. Seasonality: Consider the presence of seasonal fluctuations in sales data. Seasonal trends can influence overall sales performance and should be accounted for in forecasting models.

Practical Applications of Trend Analysis

Trend analysis offers valuable insights that can inform strategic decision-making and improve business outcomes:

1. Forecasting: By extrapolating historical trends, businesses can make accurate forecasts of future sales performance. These forecasts serve as a basis for setting targets, allocating resources, and adjusting strategies to meet demand fluctuations.

2. Identifying Growth Opportunities: Recognizing upward trends allows businesses to capitalize on emerging opportunities and invest resources in areas with high growth potential. Conversely, identifying declining trends enables proactive measures to mitigate losses and explore alternative revenue streams.

3. Performance Evaluation: Trend analysis helps evaluate the effectiveness of marketing campaigns, product launches, and other initiatives by tracking their impact on sales over time. It provides valuable feedback for refining strategies and optimizing resource allocation.

4. Risk Management: Anticipating downward trends enables businesses to identify potential risks and implement risk mitigation strategies in advance. By proactively addressing challenges, organizations can minimize the impact of adverse events on sales performance.

Case Study: Trend Analysis in Action

To illustrate the practical application of trend analysis, let's consider a case study of a retail company:

Case Study: XYZ Retail

XYZ Retail operates a chain of clothing stores and wants to improve its sales forecasting accuracy to optimize inventory management and staffing levels. The company conducts trend analysis using historical sales data from the past five years.

1. Data Collection: XYZ Retail gathers sales data for each store, including daily or weekly sales figures, promotions, and external factors such as economic conditions or competitor activities.

2. Trend Identification: Analysts use exponential smoothing to identify underlying trends in sales data while filtering out noise or short-term fluctuations. They observe a consistent upward trend in overall sales, indicating steady growth over the past few years.

3. Seasonal Adjustment: XYZ Retail identifies seasonal fluctuations in sales, with peak demand occurring during holiday seasons and back-to-school periods. Seasonal decomposition helps separate these seasonal effects from the underlying trend.

4. Forecasting: Based on the observed trend and seasonal patterns, XYZ Retail develops forecasting models to predict future sales for each store. These forecasts account for both long-term growth trends and short-term seasonal variations.

5. Decision Making: Armed with accurate sales forecasts, XYZ Retail can make informed decisions about inventory procurement, staffing levels, and marketing campaigns. They allocate resources effectively to meet anticipated demand and maximize sales opportunities.

6. Monitoring and Adaptation: XYZ Retail regularly monitors actual sales performance against forecasted figures and adjusts their strategies accordingly. They incorporate new data and market trends to refine their forecasting models and improve accuracy over time.

By leveraging trend analysis, XYZ Retail achieves significant improvements in sales forecasting accuracy, leading to better inventory management, enhanced customer satisfaction, and increased profitability.

Conclusion

Trend analysis is a powerful tool for extracting actionable insights from historical sales data and making informed predictions about future performance. By identifying and understanding trends, businesses can anticipate market dynamics, capitalize on growth opportunities, and mitigate risks effectively. Through the application of various analytical techniques and interpretation of results, organizations can harness the predictive power of trend analysis to drive sustainable growth and competitive advantage in today's dynamic business environment.

Example: Trend Analysis in Retail Sales

In this example, we'll examine historical sales data for a fictional retail store, XYZ Clothing, over a period of five years. We'll apply trend analysis techniques to identify and analyze trends in sales performance, utilizing simple moving averages (SMA) and linear regression to extract actionable insights.

Data Overview

Year	Sales (in $)
2019	350,000
2020	380,000
2021	410,000
2022	440,000
2023	470,000

Trend Analysis Using Simple Moving Averages (SMA)

To begin, let's calculate a simple moving average for a three-year period to identify trends in sales data:

- 2019-2021 SMA: (350,000 + 380,000 + 410,000) / 3 = $380,000

- 2020-2022 SMA: (380,000 + 410,000 + 440,000) / 3 = $410,000

- 2021-2023 SMA: (410,000 + 440,000 + 470,000) / 3 = $440,000

Interpretation of SMA Results

- The three-year moving average reveals an upward trend in sales, with an increase from $380,000 to $440,000 over the analyzed period.

- This indicates consistent growth in sales performance for XYZ Clothing.

Trend Analysis Using Linear Regression

Next, let's apply linear regression to the sales data to determine the slope of the trend line:

- **Linear Regression Equation:** Sales = a Year + b

Using the least squares method, we find:

- **a (slope):** 30,000 (indicating an average annual increase in sales)
- **b (y-intercept):** 185,000

Interpretation of Linear Regression Results

- The positive slope coefficient (a) of 30,000 suggests that, on average, sales increase by $30,000 per year.

- The y-intercept (b) of 185,000 represents the estimated sales at the beginning of the analysis period (2019).

- The linear regression model confirms the upward trend observed in the SMA analysis, providing a quantitative measure of sales growth.

Conclusion

Trend analysis of XYZ Clothing's sales data indicates a consistent upward trend over the five-year period, as evidenced by both simple moving averages and linear regression. This suggests that XYZ Clothing has experienced steady growth in sales performance, with an average annual increase of $30,000. Armed with this insight, XYZ Clothing can make informed decisions regarding inventory management, marketing strategies, and resource allocation to capitalize on future growth opportunities and drive sustainable business success.

4.1.3 Seasonality Considerations

Seasonality is a critical aspect of historical data analysis in sales forecasting. It refers to the recurring fluctuations or patterns that tend to appear in data at specific intervals within a year. Understanding and accounting for seasonality is essential for accurate forecasting, as sales performance can vary significantly based on factors such as holidays, weather, cultural events, and other seasonal influences. In this section, we will delve into the significance of seasonality considerations in sales metrics and analytics.

Understanding Seasonal Patterns

Seasonal patterns can manifest in various forms, depending on the nature of the business and its market. For instance, retail businesses often experience spikes in sales during holiday seasons like Christmas or back-to-school periods. Similarly, industries such as tourism may see increased demand during specific seasons like summer or winter vacations. By analyzing historical sales data, businesses can identify these recurring patterns and incorporate them into their forecasting models.

Methods for Seasonal Adjustment

To account for seasonality in sales forecasting, several methods can be employed:

1. Seasonal Decomposition

- **Additive Model:** This method involves breaking down the time series data into three main components: trend, seasonality, and random fluctuations. The seasonal component is then isolated and adjusted separately to remove its influence on the data.

- **Multiplicative Model:** Similar to the additive model, but the seasonal component is expressed as a ratio or percentage of the trend rather than an absolute value.

2. Moving Averages

- Moving averages smooth out fluctuations in data by calculating the average of a specific number of consecutive time periods. By using moving averages, seasonal effects can be minimized, allowing for a clearer view of underlying trends.

3. Seasonal Indexing

- Seasonal indexing involves creating seasonal indices that represent the relative strength of sales during different seasons compared to an average period. These indices can then be used to adjust future forecasts based on historical seasonal trends.

4. Fourier Analysis

- Fourier analysis is a mathematical technique used to decompose complex patterns into simpler sinusoidal components. By applying Fourier analysis to sales data, businesses can identify the dominant seasonal frequencies and adjust their forecasts accordingly.

Challenges in Seasonal Analysis

While accounting for seasonality is crucial for accurate sales forecasting, it also presents several challenges:

1. Data Volatility

- Seasonal patterns may change over time due to factors such as shifts in consumer behavior, economic conditions, or competitive dynamics. Consequently, historical data may not always provide a reliable indicator of future seasonality.

2. Overfitting

- Overfitting occurs when a forecasting model captures noise or random fluctuations in the data instead of genuine patterns. Seasonal adjustment techniques should be applied judiciously to avoid overfitting, which can lead to inaccurate forecasts.

3. Irregular Events

- Not all fluctuations in sales can be attributed to seasonal factors. Irregular events such as product launches, marketing campaigns, or external shocks (e.g., natural disasters) can also impact sales performance and may need to be distinguished from seasonal effects.

Best Practices for Seasonal Forecasting

To effectively incorporate seasonality into sales forecasting, businesses should adhere to the following best practices:

1. Comprehensive Data Collection

- Collect a wide range of historical data encompassing multiple years and seasons to capture diverse seasonal patterns and trends accurately.

2. Regular Model Evaluation

- Periodically evaluate forecasting models to assess their accuracy in capturing seasonal variations. Adjust models as necessary to account for evolving seasonal patterns.

3. Sensitivity Analysis

- Conduct sensitivity analysis to gauge the impact of different seasonal adjustment techniques on forecast accuracy. Identify the most suitable approach based on the specific characteristics of the business and its market.

4. Collaboration Across Functions

- Foster collaboration between sales, marketing, operations, and finance teams to ensure alignment in understanding seasonal influences on business performance. Integrate insights from different functions into the forecasting process to enhance accuracy and reliability.

Case Study: Seasonal Forecasting in Retail

Consider a retail chain specializing in outdoor recreational equipment. The company experiences significant seasonality, with sales peaking during the summer months due to increased demand for camping gear, hiking equipment, and outdoor apparel. To account for this seasonality in forecasting, the company employs a combination of seasonal decomposition and moving averages.

By decomposing historical sales data into trend and seasonal components, the company identifies the recurring patterns associated with different seasons. Moving averages are then applied to smooth out short-term fluctuations and highlight underlying trends. Additionally, the company uses seasonal indexing to adjust forecasts based on the relative strength of sales during peak seasons compared to off-peak periods.

Through rigorous data analysis and seasonal adjustment techniques, the retail chain is able to generate more accurate forecasts, optimize inventory management, and capitalize on seasonal opportunities effectively.

Conclusion

Incorporating seasonality considerations into sales forecasting is essential for businesses to anticipate and adapt to fluctuations in demand effectively. By understanding seasonal patterns, employing appropriate adjustment techniques, and adhering to best practices, organizations can enhance the accuracy and reliability of their forecasts, leading to improved decision-making and sustainable growth. As markets continue to evolve, businesses must remain vigilant in monitoring seasonal trends and adjusting their forecasting strategies accordingly to stay ahead of the curve.

Illustrative Example: Seasonality Considerations in Retail Sales Forecasting

Consider a retail chain specializing in outdoor recreational equipment with stores across the United States. The company aims to improve its sales forecasting accuracy by incorporating seasonality considerations into its analysis.

Historical Data Analysis

The company collects sales data for the past five years, broken down by month, to identify seasonal patterns in sales. Let's examine the monthly sales data for one of the company's flagship stores:

Month	Sales (in $)
January	30,000
February	35,000
March	40,000
April	45,000
May	60,000
June	75,000
July	80,000
August	85,000
September	70,000
October	55,000
November	45,000
December	65,000

Seasonal Decomposition

The company applies seasonal decomposition to the sales data using an additive model to separate the trend, seasonality, and random fluctuations. The seasonal component is then isolated to understand its impact on sales.

Using statistical software, the seasonal decomposition yields the following results:

- Trend Component: $y_t = 5000t + 30000$
- Seasonal Component:
  - January: -10,000
  - February: -5,000
  - March: 0
  - April: 5,000
  - May: 20,000
  - June: 35,000
  - July: 40,000
  - August: 45,000
  - September: 30,000
  - October: 15,000
  - November: 5,000
  - December: 25,000

Moving Averages

Next, the company applies a 12-month moving average to smooth out short-term fluctuations and highlight the underlying sales trend. The moving average calculation for each month is as follows:

- January: ($30,000 + $35,000 + ... + $65,000) / 12 = $49,167
- February: ($35,000 + $40,000 + ... + $70,000) / 12 = $52,500

- ...

- December: ($65,000 + $60,000 + ... + $35,000) / 12 = $50,833

Seasonal Adjustment

Using the seasonal indices derived from the seasonal decomposition, the company adjusts the moving averages to account for seasonal effects. The adjusted moving averages for each month are calculated by adding the seasonal component to the moving average:

- January: $49,167 - $10,000 = $39,167

- February: $52,500 - $5,000 = $47,500

- ...

- December: $50,833 + $25,000 = $75,833

Analysis

By incorporating seasonality considerations into the sales forecasting process, the company gains valuable insights into the seasonal trends driving sales performance. For instance:

- Seasonal Decomposition: The analysis reveals that sales tend to peak during the summer months (June, July, August), corresponding to the outdoor recreational season. Conversely, sales dip during the winter months (January, February), indicating reduced demand for outdoor equipment.

- Moving Averages: The moving averages smooth out short-term fluctuations, providing a clearer picture of the underlying sales trend. This enables the company to identify long-term growth patterns and make informed strategic decisions.

- Seasonal Adjustment: By adjusting the moving averages for seasonal effects, the company can better anticipate fluctuations in demand and allocate resources accordingly. For example, the company can ramp up inventory levels during peak seasons to meet customer demand more effectively.

Conclusion

Incorporating seasonality considerations into sales forecasting enables the retail chain to generate more accurate predictions and optimize its operations. By leveraging historical data analysis, seasonal decomposition, moving averages, and seasonal adjustment techniques, the company can anticipate seasonal fluctuations in sales, improve inventory management, and capitalize on seasonal opportunities effectively. This illustrates the importance of seasonality considerations in enhancing sales forecasting accuracy and driving business growth.

4.2 Predictive Modeling

4.2.1 Regression Analysis

Regression analysis is a fundamental technique in predictive modeling used to understand the relationship between one dependent variable and one or more independent variables. It is widely employed in sales forecasting to predict future outcomes based on historical data and other relevant factors. In this section, we will delve into the various aspects of regression analysis and its application in sales metrics and analytics.

Understanding Regression Analysis:

Regression analysis aims to find the best-fitting relationship between a dependent variable (often denoted as Y) and one or more independent variables (often denoted as X). The relationship is typically represented by a mathematical equation of the form:

$$Y = \beta_0 + \beta_1 X_1 + \beta_2 X_2 + \ldots + \beta_n X_n + \varepsilon$$

Where:

- Y is the dependent variable (e.g., sales revenue).

- $X_1, X_2, \ldots, X_n$ are independent variables (e.g., advertising expenditure, time).

- $\beta_0, \beta_1, \beta_2, \ldots, \beta_n$ are the coefficients that represent the strength and direction of the relationship between the variables.

- ε is the error term, representing the difference between the observed and predicted values.

The goal of regression analysis is to estimate the coefficients (β) that minimize the error term, thus providing the best-fit line or plane that describes the relationship between the variables.

Types of Regression Analysis:

Regression analysis encompasses various techniques, each suited to different types of data and modeling objectives. Some common types include:

1. Simple Linear Regression: Involves a single independent variable and a linear relationship with the dependent variable.

2. Multiple Linear Regression: Extends simple linear regression to include multiple independent variables.

3. Polynomial Regression: Accommodates non-linear relationships by introducing polynomial terms into the regression equation.

4. Logistic Regression: Used when the dependent variable is categorical, estimating the probability of a binary outcome.

Application in Sales Forecasting:

Regression analysis plays a crucial role in sales forecasting by enabling businesses to identify and quantify the factors influencing sales performance. Here's how it is applied:

1. Demand Estimation:

By analyzing historical sales data along with relevant variables such as pricing, marketing efforts, and economic indicators, regression models can forecast future demand for a product or service.

2. Price Optimization:

Regression analysis helps businesses determine the optimal price point by assessing the impact of pricing on sales volume and revenue. It identifies the price elasticity of demand, indicating how sensitive customers are to price changes.

3. Marketing Effectiveness:

Regression models evaluate the effectiveness of marketing campaigns by examining the relationship between marketing expenditure and sales outcomes. This helps in allocating resources efficiently across different marketing channels.

4. Seasonal Variation Analysis:

Regression analysis can capture seasonal patterns in sales data, enabling businesses to adjust their strategies accordingly. By incorporating seasonal variables, such as time of year or holidays, the model can provide more accurate forecasts.

Challenges and Considerations:

While regression analysis offers valuable insights, it also poses certain challenges and considerations:

- **Assumption Violation:** Regression models rely on several assumptions, such as linearity, independence of errors, and homoscedasticity. Violations of these assumptions can lead to biased or unreliable results.

- **Overfitting:** Including too many independent variables or complex polynomial terms can result in overfitting, where the model performs well on the training data but fails to generalize to new data.

- **Multicollinearity:** When independent variables are highly correlated, multicollinearity can occur, leading to unstable coefficient estimates and difficulties in interpreting the model.

- **Outliers and Influential Points:** Outliers and influential points can distort the regression line and affect the accuracy of predictions. Robust regression techniques or data transformations may be needed to address these issues.

Conclusion:

Regression analysis is a powerful tool in sales metrics and analytics, offering a systematic approach to understanding and predicting sales performance. By leveraging historical data and relevant variables, businesses can develop robust regression models to inform strategic decision-making, optimize resources, and drive growth. However, it is essential to approach regression analysis with caution, considering its assumptions, limitations, and potential challenges to ensure accurate and reliable results.

Illustrative Example: Regression Analysis in Sales Forecasting

Background:

Imagine a retail company, XYZ Corp, specializing in electronics, aiming to forecast its sales revenue for the upcoming quarter. The company has historical data on sales revenue, advertising expenditure, and promotional activities over the past few years. They want to leverage regression analysis to understand how these factors influence sales and make accurate predictions for the next quarter.

Data:

1. Sales Revenue (dependent variable):

   - Quarter 1: $500,000

   - Quarter 2: $550,000

   - Quarter 3: $600,000

   - Quarter 4: $620,000

2. Advertising Expenditure (in thousands of dollars):

   - Quarter 1: $50

   - Quarter 2: $60

   - Quarter 3: $55

   - Quarter 4: $65

3. Promotional Activities (binary variable):

   - Quarter 1: Yes

   - Quarter 2: Yes

   - Quarter 3: No

   - Quarter 4: Yes

Regression Analysis:

We will conduct a multiple linear regression analysis using sales revenue as the dependent variable and advertising expenditure and promotional activities as independent variables.

Sales Revenue = $\beta_0 + \beta_1 \times$ Advertising Expenditure + $\beta_2 \times$ Promotional Activities + ε

Model Estimation:

Using statistical software, we estimate the coefficients (β) of the regression model:

- β_0 (Intercept) = $400,000
- β_1 (Advertising Expenditure) = $5,000
- β_2 (Promotional Activities) = $20,000

The regression equation becomes:

Sales Revenue = 400,000 + 5,000 x times Advertising Expenditure + 20,000 x Promotional Activities + ε

Interpretation:

1. Advertising Expenditure Coefficient β_1:

- Holding other variables constant, a one-unit increase in advertising expenditure (in thousands of dollars) is associated with a $5,000 increase in sales revenue.

2. Promotional Activities Coefficient β_2:

- Holding other variables constant, conducting promotional activities is associated with a $20,000 increase in sales revenue compared to not conducting promotional activities.

Sales Forecasting:

Using the regression equation, we can forecast sales revenue for the next quarter:

- **Quarter 1 Forecast:**

  - Advertising Expenditure: $70,000

  - Promotional Activities: Yes

$$Sales\ Revenue = 400{,}000 + 5{,}000 \times 70 + 20{,}000 \times 1 = \$775{,}000$$

Analysis:

- **Impact of Advertising Expenditure:** The regression analysis suggests that increasing advertising expenditure by $1,000 is associated with an additional $5,000 in sales revenue, indicating a positive and significant relationship.

- **Effectiveness of Promotional Activities:** The coefficient for promotional activities indicates that conducting promotions adds $20,000 to sales revenue. This highlights the importance of promotional strategies in driving sales growth.

- **Forecast Accuracy:** By incorporating advertising expenditure and promotional activities into the regression model, XYZ Corp can make more accurate sales forecasts, enabling them to allocate resources effectively and capitalize on revenue opportunities.

Conclusion:

This illustrative example demonstrates how regression analysis can be applied in sales forecasting to understand the impact of advertising expenditure and promotional activities on sales revenue. By estimating the coefficients and interpreting the results, businesses like XYZ Corp can make informed decisions to optimize their marketing strategies and drive revenue growth.

4.2.2 Machine Learning Algorithms

Machine learning algorithms play a pivotal role in predictive modeling within sales forecasting. These algorithms are designed to learn from historical data and patterns to make predictions or decisions without being explicitly programmed. In the realm of sales forecasting, machine learning algorithms offer a diverse set of tools to analyze complex data relationships, uncover insights, and generate accurate predictions. In this section, we delve into some of the prominent machine learning algorithms utilized in sales forecasting and discuss their applications, strengths, and limitations.

Linear Regression

Linear regression is one of the simplest and most widely used machine learning algorithms for predictive modeling in sales forecasting. It works on the principle of fitting a linear equation to observed data, with the goal of predicting the value of a dependent variable based on one or more independent variables. In the context of sales forecasting, linear regression can be employed to establish relationships between sales and various factors such as advertising expenditure, pricing strategies, and economic indicators. By analyzing historical sales data alongside relevant variables, linear regression models can provide valuable insights into the factors driving sales performance and help forecast future sales trends.

Applications: Linear regression is particularly useful for analyzing straightforward relationships between sales and independent variables, making it suitable for scenarios where the relationship is expected to be linear or can be approximated as such. It is commonly used in retail forecasting, where factors like seasonality, promotions, and pricing influence sales patterns.

Strengths:

- **Interpretability:** Linear regression models are easy to interpret, as they provide coefficients that indicate the strength and direction of the relationship between variables.

- **Computational Efficiency:** Training and inference with linear regression models are computationally efficient, making them suitable for large datasets.

- **Simple Implementation:** Linear regression models have a straightforward implementation, making them accessible even to users with limited machine learning expertise.

Limitations:

- **Assumption of Linearity:** Linear regression assumes a linear relationship between the dependent and independent variables, which may not always hold true in real-world scenarios.

- **Limited Flexibility**: Linear regression models have limited flexibility in capturing complex nonlinear relationships between variables.

- **Vulnerability to Outliers:** Linear regression can be sensitive to outliers in the data, potentially affecting the model's accuracy and reliability.

Decision Trees

Decision trees are hierarchical tree structures that recursively partition the data into subsets based on the values of different attributes, with the aim of maximizing the homogeneity of the target variable within each subset. In sales forecasting, decision trees can be employed to identify significant factors influencing sales outcomes and make predictions based on decision rules derived from historical data. Decision trees are particularly adept at handling categorical variables and interactions between predictors, making them valuable tools for exploring complex sales datasets.

Applications: Decision trees are widely used in sales forecasting applications where the relationships between predictors and sales outcomes are nonlinear or involve interactions between multiple variables. They are effective for analyzing datasets with a mix of categorical and numerical features, such as customer demographics, product attributes, and marketing channels.

Strengths:

- **Interpretability:** Decision trees offer a transparent and interpretable representation of decision rules, making it easy to understand the factors driving sales predictions.

- **Handling Nonlinear Relationships:** Decision trees can capture nonlinear relationships between predictors and sales outcomes, allowing for more flexible modeling of complex datasets.

- **Feature Importance:** Decision trees provide insights into the relative importance of different predictors in influencing sales performance, aiding in feature selection and prioritization.

Limitations:

- **Overfitting:** Decision trees are prone to overfitting, especially when dealing with noisy or high-dimensional data. Techniques such as pruning and ensemble methods (e.g., random forests) can help mitigate this issue.

- **Instability:** Small variations in the training data can lead to different tree structures, making decision trees relatively unstable compared to other algorithms.

- **Limited Predictive Power:** Decision trees may struggle to capture subtle patterns or relationships in the data, particularly when dealing with sparse or imbalanced datasets.

Random Forests

Random forests are ensemble learning algorithms that combine the predictions of multiple individual decision trees to improve accuracy and robustness. Each tree in the random forest is trained on a bootstrapped sample of the training data, and feature subsets are randomly selected for each split, reducing the correlation between individual trees. By aggregating the predictions of multiple trees, random forests can offer higher predictive performance and better generalization than individual decision trees, making them a popular choice for sales forecasting tasks.

Applications: Random forests are well-suited for sales forecasting applications where predictive accuracy and robustness are paramount. They excel in scenarios with complex, high-dimensional data and are effective at handling noise, outliers, and interactions between predictors.

Strengths:

- **High Predictive Accuracy:** Random forests typically yield higher predictive accuracy compared to individual decision trees, thanks to the ensemble nature of the algorithm.

- **Robustness:** Random forests are robust to overfitting and noise, making them suitable for noisy or high-dimensional datasets commonly encountered in sales forecasting.

- **Feature Importance:** Random forests provide measures of feature importance, enabling analysts to identify the most influential predictors in driving sales performance.

Limitations:

- **Computational Complexity:** Random forests can be computationally expensive to train and evaluate, particularly for large datasets or a large number of trees in the ensemble.

- **Lack of Interpretability:** While random forests offer high predictive accuracy, the resulting models are often less interpretable than individual decision trees due to the ensemble nature of the algorithm.

- **Parameter Tuning:** Random forests involve several hyperparameters that need to be tuned to optimize performance, which can require extensive experimentation and computational resources.

Gradient Boosting Machines (GBM)

Gradient boosting machines (GBM) are a class of ensemble learning algorithms that build predictive models in a sequential fashion, where each new model corrects the errors made by the previous ones. GBM sequentially adds weak learners (typically decision trees) to the ensemble, with each tree focusing on the residuals or errors of the previous predictions. By iteratively refining the model based on the residuals, GBM can effectively capture complex relationships in the data and produce highly accurate predictions.

Applications: GBM algorithms are widely used in sales forecasting applications where predictive accuracy is paramount and interpretability is less critical. They excel in scenarios with complex, nonlinear relationships and large amounts of data, making them suitable for high-dimensional sales datasets.

Strengths:

- **High Predictive Accuracy:** GBM algorithms typically yield state-of-the-art predictive performance, often outperforming other machine learning algorithms on a wide range of datasets.

- **Flexibility:** GBM can capture complex, nonlinear relationships between predictors and sales outcomes, making them well-suited for modeling diverse sales datasets.

- **Feature Importance:** GBM provide insights into the relative importance of different predictors in driving sales performance, aiding in feature selection and interpretation.

Limitations:

- **Computational Complexity:** GBM algorithms can be computationally intensive to train, particularly for large datasets or complex models with many iterations.

- **Overfitting:** GBM are prone to overfitting, especially when the number of iterations or the depth of the trees is not properly tuned. Regularization techniques can help mitigate this issue.

- **Parameter Sensitivity:** GBM involve several hyperparameters that need to be carefully tuned to optimize performance, which can require extensive experimentation and computational resources.

Neural Networks

Neural networks, particularly deep learning architectures, have gained prominence in recent years due to their ability to learn complex patterns from data without the need for manual feature engineering. In the context of sales forecasting, neural networks can be used to model nonlinear relationships between predictors and sales outcomes, capture temporal dependencies in time-series data, and extract valuable insights from large-scale datasets. Deep learning architectures such as recurrent neural networks (RNNs) and convolutional neural networks (CNNs) have shown promise in sales forecasting tasks, offering high predictive accuracy and the ability to handle diverse data modalities.

Applications: Neural networks are suitable for a wide range of sales forecasting applications, including demand forecasting, revenue prediction, and customer churn prediction. They excel in scenarios with large volumes of data, complex relationships, and temporal dependencies.

Strengths:

- **Nonlinear Modeling:** Neural networks can model complex, nonlinear relationships between predictors and sales outcomes, making them suitable for a wide range of forecasting tasks.

- **Temporal Modeling:** Recurrent neural networks (RNNs) are adept at capturing temporal dependencies in time-series data, allowing for more accurate predictions of sales trends and patterns.

- **Feature Learning:** Neural networks can automatically learn relevant features from raw data, eliminating the need for manual feature engineering and potentially uncovering hidden patterns or insights.

Limitations:

- **Data Requirements:** Neural networks typically require large amounts of data to train effectively, which may be a limitation in scenarios with limited or sparse data.

- **Computational Resources:** Training deep neural networks can be computationally intensive, particularly for complex architectures and large datasets.

- **Interpretability:** Neural networks are often considered black-box models, making it challenging to interpret the underlying reasons behind their predictions and insights.

Support Vector Machines (SVM)

Support vector machines (SVM) are supervised learning algorithms that excel in binary classification tasks by finding the hyperplane that best separates data points into different classes. In the context of sales forecasting, SVM can be adapted for regression tasks to predict continuous sales outcomes based on input features. SVM aim to maximize the margin between data points of different classes, allowing for robust generalization to unseen data and improved predictive performance.

Applications: SVM algorithms are suitable for sales forecasting tasks where the relationship between predictors and sales outcomes is nonlinear and the data is well-structured and labeled. They are particularly effective for scenarios with small to medium-sized datasets and a moderate number of features.

Strengths:

- **Robustness:** SVM aim to maximize the margin between different classes, making them robust to outliers and noise in the data.

- **Nonlinear Modeling**: SVM can capture complex, nonlinear relationships between predictors and sales outcomes using kernel functions, such as radial basis function (RBF) kernels.

- **Generalization:** SVM seek to find the hyperplane that best separates different classes, leading to improved generalization performance on unseen data.

Limitations:

- **Scalability:** SVM algorithms may struggle with scalability when dealing with large-scale datasets, as the computational complexity grows quadratically with the number of data points.

- **Parameter Sensitivity:** SVM involve several hyperparameters that need to be carefully tuned to optimize performance, which can be challenging and time-consuming.

- **Interpretability:** SVM models are often considered black-box models, making it difficult to interpret the underlying reasons behind their predictions and insights.

Conclusion

In the realm of sales forecasting, predictive modeling using machine learning algorithms offers a powerful toolkit for analyzing historical data, uncovering insights, and making accurate predictions. From traditional techniques like linear regression to state-of-the-art approaches such as neural networks and gradient boosting machines, a diverse array of algorithms are available to tackle various forecasting challenges. By understanding the strengths, limitations, and applications of different machine learning algorithms, organizations can harness the power of data-driven insights to optimize sales performance, identify growth opportunities, and stay ahead of the competition. As technology continues to evolve and datasets grow in complexity, the role of machine learning in sales forecasting is poised to become even more indispensable, driving innovation and driving business success in the dynamic landscape of sales and marketing.

4.2.3 Forecast Accuracy Metrics

Forecast accuracy metrics are essential for assessing the performance of predictive models. They provide insights into how well the model's forecasts align with actual outcomes, allowing businesses to identify areas for improvement and refine their forecasting strategies. Below are some commonly used forecast accuracy metrics:

1. Mean Absolute Error (MAE):

The Mean Absolute Error measures the average magnitude of errors between predicted and actual values. It is calculated by taking the average of the absolute differences between forecasted and observed values.

$$MAE = \frac{1}{n} \sum_{i=1}^{n} |Y_i - \hat{Y}_i|$$

Where:

- Y_i represents the actual value.

- $\hat{Y}_i$ represents the forecasted value.

- n is the total number of observations.

A lower MAE indicates better accuracy, with values closer to zero indicating minimal error.

2. Mean Squared Error (MSE):

The Mean Squared Error measures the average of the squared differences between predicted and actual values. It penalizes larger errors more heavily than smaller ones.

$$MSE = \frac{1}{n} \sum_{i=1}^{n} (Y_i - \hat{Y}_i)^2$$

MSE provides a measure of the variability of prediction errors. Like MAE, lower values of MSE indicate better accuracy.

3. Root Mean Squared Error (RMSE):

The Root Mean Squared Error is the square root of the Mean Squared Error. It is more interpretable as it is in the same units as the original data.

$$RMSE = \sqrt{\frac{1}{n} \sum_{i=1}^{n}(Y_i - \hat{Y}_i)^2}$$

RMSE is widely used in forecasting evaluation and provides a good measure of model performance.

4. Mean Absolute Percentage Error (MAPE):

The Mean Absolute Percentage Error calculates the average percentage difference between predicted and actual values. It is particularly useful when dealing with data with varying scales.

$$MAPE = \frac{1}{n} \sum_{i=1}^{n} \left| \frac{Y_i - \hat{Y}_i}{Y_i} \right| \times 100\%$$

MAPE expresses forecast errors as a percentage of actual values, making it easy to interpret. However, it is sensitive to zero values and can be misleading when dealing with small denominators.

5. Forecast Bias:

Forecast Bias measures the tendency of a model to consistently over- or under-forecast. It is calculated as the average of forecast errors, with positive values indicating over-forecasting and negative values indicating under-forecasting.

$$ForecastBias = \frac{1}{n} \sum_{i=1}^{n}(Y_i - \hat{Y}_i)$$

Identifying and correcting bias in forecasts is crucial for improving model accuracy and reliability.

6. Theil's U Statistic:

Theil's U Statistic compares the accuracy of the forecasted values to a naïve model, such as a simple moving average. It measures the ratio of the root mean squared forecast error to the root mean squared error of the naïve model.

$$U = \sqrt{\frac{\sum_{t=1}^{n}(Y_t - \hat{Y}_t)^2}{\sum_{t=1}^{n}(Y_t - \overline{Y})^2}}$$

Where:

- Y_t represents the actual value at time t

- $\hat{Y}_t$ represents the forecasted value at time t

- $\overline{Y}$ represents the mean of actual values.

A value of U close to 1 indicates that the model performs similarly to the naïve model, while values less than 1 indicate better performance.

7. Symmetric Mean Absolute Percentage Error (sMAPE):

The Symmetric Mean Absolute Percentage Error calculates the average percentage difference between predicted and actual values, taking into account the scale of the data. Unlike MAPE, it treats over- and under-forecasting symmetrically.

$$sMAPE = \frac{1}{n}\sum_{i=1}^{n} \frac{2|Y_i - \hat{Y}_i|}{|Y_i| + |\hat{Y}_i|} \times 100\%$$

sMAPE provides a balanced measure of forecast accuracy and is suitable for comparing performance across different datasets.

Conclusion:

Forecast accuracy metrics play a crucial role in evaluating the effectiveness of predictive models. By systematically analyzing forecast errors and performance indicators, businesses can refine their forecasting strategies, improve decision-making, and drive growth. It is essential to select appropriate metrics based on the characteristics of the data and the specific objectives of the forecasting task. Continuous monitoring and validation of models against actual outcomes are also vital to ensure their reliability and relevance in dynamic business environments.

Example: Forecast Accuracy Evaluation Using Mean Absolute Error (MAE)

Let's consider a fictional scenario where a retail company, XYZ Retail, is forecasting its monthly sales for the next year. The company has historical sales data for the past three years and wants to assess the accuracy of its forecasting model using the Mean Absolute Error (MAE) metric.

Historical Sales Data:

Month	Actual Sales ($ millions)
Jan	2.5
Feb	3.0

Mar	2.8
Apr	3.2
May	3.5
Jun	3.7
Jul	4.0
Aug	4.2
Sep	3.9
Oct	3.6
Nov	3.3
Dec	3.1

Forecasted Sales for the Next Year:

Assume XYZ Retail has developed a predictive model based on historical data and has generated forecasted sales for the next year as follows:

Month	Forecasted Sales ($ millions)
Jan	2.7
Feb	3.1
Mar	2.9
Apr	3.4
May	3.6
Jun	3.8
Jul	4.1
Aug	4.0
Sep	3.8
Oct	3.5
Nov	3.2
Dec	3.0

Calculation of Mean Absolute Error (MAE):

To evaluate the accuracy of the forecasting model, we calculate the Mean Absolute Error (MAE) using the formula:

$$MAE = \frac{1}{n} \sum_{i=1}^{n} |Y_i - \hat{Y}_i|$$

Where:

- Y_i represents the actual sales for month i

- $\hat{Y}_i$ represents the forecasted sales for month i

- n is the total number of months.

Using the provided data, let's calculate MAE:

MAE = [|2.5 - 2.7| + |3.0 - 3.1| + ... + |3.1 - 3.0|] / 12}

MAE = (0.2 + 0.1 + ... + 0.1)/12

MAE = 1.4/12]

MAE = 0.1167

Evaluation:

The calculated MAE is 0.1167 million dollars. This indicates that, on average, the forecasted sales deviate from the actual sales by approximately $116,700. A lower MAE value suggests better accuracy, so in this case, the forecasting model has performed reasonably well, with relatively small errors in predicting monthly sales.

Overall, while MAE provides a useful measure of forecast accuracy, it is essential to consider other metrics and qualitative factors to comprehensively evaluate the performance of predictive models and identify areas for improvement.

4.3 Market Trends Analysis

Market trends analysis is a crucial aspect of sales forecasting and strategic decision-making for any business. Understanding the dynamics of the market landscape allows companies to identify opportunities, anticipate challenges, and stay ahead of competitors. In this section, we delve into the importance of competitor analysis as a fundamental component of market trends analysis.

4.3.1 Competitor Analysis

Competitor analysis involves evaluating the strengths and weaknesses of current and potential competitors to inform business strategy. By gaining insights into competitors' actions, capabilities, and performance, companies can benchmark their own performance, identify areas for improvement, and devise effective strategies to gain a competitive advantage.

Why Competitor Analysis Matters

1. Identifying Market Opportunities and Threats: By monitoring competitors' activities, businesses can identify emerging trends, market gaps, and potential threats. This insight enables proactive decision-making and helps businesses capitalize on opportunities before competitors do.

2. Understanding Competitive Positioning: Analyzing competitors' products, pricing strategies, distribution channels, and marketing tactics provides valuable insights into how they position themselves in the market. This understanding helps businesses refine their own positioning and differentiation strategies to stand out in the crowded marketplace.

3. Benchmarking Performance: Comparing key performance indicators (KPIs) such as market share, sales growth, profitability, and customer satisfaction against competitors allows businesses to assess their relative performance and identify areas where they excel or lag behind. This benchmarking facilitates setting realistic goals and performance targets.

4. Anticipating Competitive Moves: By monitoring competitors' announcements, product launches, marketing campaigns, and strategic partnerships, businesses can anticipate their next moves and prepare appropriate responses. This proactive approach helps businesses stay agile and responsive in a competitive environment.

5. Improving Product Development: Analyzing competitors' products and customer feedback provides valuable insights for enhancing product features, functionality, and user experience. This iterative process of learning from competitors' successes and failures enables businesses to deliver more innovative and customer-centric solutions.

Key Components of Competitor Analysis

1. Competitor Identification: Begin by identifying direct and indirect competitors operating in the same market segment or targeting similar customer segments. Direct competitors offer similar products or services, while indirect competitors may serve different needs but compete for the same budget or resources.

2. Competitive Profiling: Once competitors are identified, gather comprehensive information about their business models, target markets, product offerings, pricing strategies, distribution channels, marketing tactics, and key personnel. This information can be obtained through primary research, secondary research, industry reports, and competitor websites.

3. SWOT Analysis: Conduct a SWOT (Strengths, Weaknesses, Opportunities, Threats) analysis for each competitor to assess their relative strengths and weaknesses compared to your own business. This analysis helps identify areas where competitors excel and areas where they may be vulnerable.

4. Market Positioning Analysis: Evaluate how competitors position themselves in the market relative to factors such as product quality, price, convenience, brand reputation, and customer service. This analysis helps identify gaps in the market and opportunities for differentiation.

5. Performance Metrics Comparison: Compare key performance metrics such as market share, sales growth, profitability, customer satisfaction, and brand awareness across competitors. This comparison provides insights into relative market dynamics and competitive intensity.

6. Trend Analysis: Monitor long-term trends in competitors' performance, market share, customer preferences, technological advancements, regulatory changes, and macroeconomic indicators. This analysis helps identify emerging opportunities and threats in the market.

7. Competitive Response Planning: Based on the insights gained from competitor analysis, develop strategic response plans to counter competitive threats, capitalize on market opportunities, and strengthen your competitive position. These plans may involve adjustments to product features, pricing strategies, marketing campaigns, distribution channels, or partnerships.

Tools and Techniques for Competitor Analysis

1. Market Research Surveys: Conduct surveys among customers, prospects, and industry experts to gather feedback on competitors' products, services, and brand perceptions.

2. Mystery Shopping: Engage in mystery shopping to evaluate competitors' customer service, sales processes, and product offerings from a customer perspective.

3. Competitor Intelligence Platforms: Utilize specialized software tools and services that provide real-time data and analysis on competitors' online activities, advertising campaigns, social media engagement, and website traffic.

4. Financial Analysis: Review competitors' financial statements, annual reports, and SEC filings to assess their financial health, revenue growth, profitability, and investment priorities.

5. Patent and Trademark Searches: Conduct searches on patent and trademark databases to identify competitors' intellectual property assets, innovations, and R&D priorities.

6. Industry Conferences and Events: Attend industry conferences, trade shows, and networking events to gather intelligence on competitors' product launches, partnerships, and strategic initiatives.

7. Competitive Benchmarking: Engage in formal benchmarking exercises to compare your performance against industry peers and best-in-class competitors across various metrics.

Case Study: Competitor Analysis in Action

Let's illustrate the importance of competitor analysis with a case study of a consumer electronics company planning to launch a new smartphone product.

1. Competitor Identification: The company identifies several major competitors in the smartphone market, including Apple, Samsung, Huawei, Xiaomi, and OnePlus.

2. Competitive Profiling: The company gathers detailed information about each competitor's product lineup, pricing strategy, distribution channels, marketing campaigns, and customer reviews.

3. SWOT Analysis: The company conducts a SWOT analysis for each competitor, identifying their strengths (e.g., strong brand reputation, innovative features), weaknesses (e.g., high pricing, limited distribution), opportunities (e.g., emerging markets, growing demand for 5G phones), and threats (e.g., intense competition, regulatory challenges).

4. Market Positioning Analysis: The company evaluates how competitors position their smartphones in terms of features, performance, design, pricing, and target audience. This analysis helps the company identify opportunities to differentiate its own product and messaging.

5. Performance Metrics Comparison: The company compares key performance metrics such as market share, sales volume, customer satisfaction ratings, and online reviews across competitors. This comparison highlights areas where competitors excel and areas where the company can gain a competitive edge.

6. Trend Analysis: The company monitors trends in competitors' product launches, technology innovations, marketing strategies, and pricing adjustments. This analysis helps the company anticipate market shifts and adjust its product roadmap accordingly.

7. Competitive Response Planning: Based on the insights gained from competitor analysis, the company develops a strategic response plan that focuses on offering unique features, aggressive pricing, exclusive partnerships, and targeted marketing campaigns to differentiate its smartphone product and capture market share.

Conclusion

Competitor analysis is a fundamental aspect of market trends analysis that provides businesses with valuable insights into the competitive landscape. By understanding competitors' strengths, weaknesses, strategies, and performance, companies can identify opportunities, anticipate threats, and devise effective strategies to gain a competitive advantage. Incorporating competitor analysis into the sales forecasting process enables businesses to make informed decisions, mitigate risks, and achieve sustainable growth in dynamic markets.

Through continuous monitoring and analysis of competitors' actions and market dynamics, businesses can adapt their strategies in real-time to stay ahead of the competition and drive long-term success.

4.3.2 Industry Research

In the ever-evolving landscape of sales, staying ahead requires not only an understanding of your own company's performance but also a keen awareness of broader industry trends. Industry research forms the backbone of informed decision-making, enabling businesses to anticipate changes, capitalize on emerging opportunities, and mitigate risks. This section delves into the methodologies and importance of industry research within the realm of sales metrics and analytics.

Importance of Industry Research

Industry research serves as a compass guiding businesses through the complex terrain of market dynamics. By analyzing industry trends, companies gain valuable insights into consumer behavior, competitive landscapes, regulatory developments, technological advancements, and economic shifts. These insights empower organizations to align their strategies with prevailing market conditions, fostering adaptability and resilience.

Strategic Planning

Industry research underpins strategic planning by providing a comprehensive understanding of market forces. Whether entering a new market segment or refining existing offerings, businesses rely on industry insights to make informed decisions. By identifying emerging trends and consumer preferences, organizations can tailor their strategies to meet evolving demands effectively.

Competitive Analysis

Understanding competitors is crucial for maintaining a competitive edge. Industry research facilitates competitive analysis by evaluating rivals' strengths, weaknesses, market positioning, and strategies. By benchmarking against industry peers, businesses can identify areas for improvement and differentiation, informing strategic initiatives such as product development, pricing strategies, and marketing campaigns.

Risk Mitigation

Navigating uncertainties requires a proactive approach to risk management. Industry research enables businesses to anticipate potential threats, such as regulatory changes, economic downturns, or disruptive technologies. By staying abreast of industry developments, organizations can devise contingency plans and mitigate risks effectively, safeguarding against adverse impacts on sales performance.

Methodologies of Industry Research

Conducting effective industry research entails a systematic approach encompassing various methodologies and data sources. From primary research involving direct engagement with stakeholders to secondary research leveraging existing data sources, organizations employ diverse methods to gain actionable insights into market trends.

Primary Research

Primary research involves gathering firsthand information from industry stakeholders, including customers, suppliers, and industry experts. Techniques such as surveys, interviews, focus groups, and observations provide valuable qualitative and quantitative data. By directly engaging with key stakeholders, businesses gain nuanced insights into market dynamics, consumer preferences, and emerging trends, enhancing the depth and accuracy of their analyses.

Surveys

Surveys are a common primary research method employed to collect quantitative data on consumer preferences, market trends, and competitive landscapes. Through structured questionnaires administered to target demographics, businesses can obtain valuable insights into purchasing behavior, product satisfaction, brand perception, and market demand. Surveys enable organizations to gauge market sentiment, identify emerging trends, and validate hypotheses, informing strategic decision-making processes.

Interviews

Interviews offer a qualitative approach to primary research, allowing businesses to delve deeper into consumer motivations, preferences, and pain points. Conducted either in person or through virtual platforms, interviews provide a platform for open-ended discussions with selected participants, such as industry experts, thought leaders, or target customers. By eliciting rich, contextual insights, interviews complement quantitative data from surveys, offering a holistic view of market dynamics and informing strategic initiatives.

Secondary Research

Secondary research involves analyzing existing data sources, including published reports, industry publications, academic journals, and online databases. By synthesizing information from diverse sources, businesses gain comprehensive insights into market trends, competitive landscapes, and macroeconomic indicators. Secondary research supplements primary data collection efforts, providing context, validation, and broader perspectives on industry dynamics.

Market Reports

Market reports published by research firms, industry associations, and government agencies offer valuable insights into market trends, growth forecasts, competitive landscapes, and regulatory developments. These reports provide quantitative data, qualitative analysis, and strategic recommendations tailored to specific industries, segments, and regions. By leveraging market reports, businesses can gain a deeper understanding of market dynamics, identify growth opportunities, and benchmark their performance against industry peers.

Industry Publications

Industry publications such as trade journals, magazines, and newsletters serve as invaluable sources of industry-specific insights, trends, and best practices. Covering a wide range of topics, from emerging technologies to regulatory changes, industry publications provide timely and relevant information to industry stakeholders. By staying abreast of industry publications, businesses can track market trends, competitive developments, and innovations, informing strategic decision-making and staying ahead of the curve.

Online Databases

Online databases offer a wealth of data and information spanning various industries, markets, and regions. From statistical databases providing macroeconomic indicators to industry-specific portals offering market research reports, online databases serve as valuable resources for industry research. By accessing relevant data sources, businesses can conduct in-depth analyses, track market trends, and identify growth opportunities, enhancing their competitive advantage and decision-making capabilities.

Challenges and Considerations

While industry research offers invaluable insights into market dynamics, it presents certain challenges and considerations that businesses must address to derive maximum value from their analyses.

Data Quality and Reliability

Ensuring the quality and reliability of data is paramount for meaningful analysis. Inaccurate or outdated data can lead to flawed conclusions and misinformed decisions. Businesses must validate data sources, verify data integrity, and assess the credibility of information sources to mitigate the risk of erroneous insights. Additionally, reconciling discrepancies between different data sources and methodologies is essential for ensuring consistency and accuracy in analyses.

Information Overload

The proliferation of data sources and information channels can overwhelm businesses, leading to information overload. With vast amounts of data available, organizations must prioritize relevant information, filter out noise, and focus on actionable insights. Employing data analytics tools and techniques such as data visualization, pattern recognition, and predictive modeling can help distill complex data sets into actionable intelligence, enabling informed decision-making and strategic planning.

Evolving Market Dynamics

The rapid pace of change in today's markets necessitates continuous monitoring and adaptation. Industry trends, consumer preferences, and competitive landscapes evolve rapidly, requiring businesses to stay agile and responsive. Static analyses may quickly become outdated, rendering strategic plans obsolete. To address this challenge, organizations must adopt a dynamic approach to industry research, leveraging real-time data, predictive analytics, and scenario planning to anticipate changes and adjust strategies proactively.

Case Study: Leveraging Industry Research for Strategic Growth

To illustrate the practical application of industry research in driving strategic growth, let us consider a hypothetical case study of a technology company expanding into the electric vehicle (EV) market.

Situation

A technology company specializing in renewable energy solutions seeks to diversify its product portfolio by entering the rapidly growing electric vehicle market. With increasing consumer interest in electric vehicles driven by environmental concerns and government incentives, the company sees an opportunity to capitalize on this trend and expand its market reach.

Approach

To inform its entry strategy into the EV market, the company conducts comprehensive industry research to assess market dynamics, competitive landscapes, and growth opportunities.

Primary Research

The company conducts interviews with industry experts, electric vehicle manufacturers, and potential customers to gain insights into market trends, consumer preferences, and competitive positioning. Through structured interviews and focus groups, the company gathers qualitative data on factors influencing EV adoption, such as charging infrastructure, range anxiety, and cost considerations.

Secondary Research

In parallel, the company leverages secondary research sources, including market reports, industry publications, and online databases, to gather

quantitative data on market size, growth projections, regulatory developments, and competitive analysis. By synthesizing information from diverse sources, the company gains a comprehensive understanding of the EV market landscape, identifying key players, market segments, and growth drivers.

Insights

Based on its industry research findings, the company identifies several key insights that inform its strategic approach to entering the EV market:

- Market Potential: Industry research reveals significant growth potential in the EV market, driven by increasing consumer demand, government incentives, and technological advancements.

- Competitive Landscape: Analysis of competitors highlights the presence of established automakers, niche players, and new entrants vying for market share. The company identifies opportunities to differentiate its offerings through innovation, performance, and sustainability.

- Consumer Preferences: Primary research findings shed light on consumer preferences for EV features such as range, charging infrastructure, and price affordability. The company incorporates these insights into its product development and marketing strategies to address customer needs effectively.

- Regulatory Environment: Industry research highlights evolving regulations and policies promoting electric vehicle adoption, including emission standards, incentives for electric vehicle purchases, and investments in charging infrastructure. The company aligns its strategy with regulatory trends to capitalize on government support and compliance requirements.

Strategy

Armed with actionable insights from industry research, the company develops a strategic roadmap for entering the EV market:

- Product Development: The company focuses on developing innovative electric vehicle solutions tailored to consumer needs and market trends. By leveraging its expertise in renewable energy technologies, the company aims to differentiate its offerings through advanced battery technology, sustainable materials, and energy-efficient designs.

- Market Segmentation: Based on market research findings, the company identifies target customer segments, including environmentally conscious consumers, fleet operators, and urban commuters. By tailoring its marketing messages and product offerings to specific market segments, the company aims to maximize its market penetration and customer acquisition.

- Partnership and Collaboration: Recognizing the importance of ecosystem partnerships, the company explores collaboration opportunities with electric vehicle manufacturers, charging infrastructure providers, and energy utilities. Strategic alliances enable the company to leverage complementary strengths, expand its market reach, and accelerate innovation in the electric vehicle ecosystem.

- Brand Positioning: Building brand credibility and trust is essential for success in the competitive EV market. The company leverages its reputation as a trusted provider of renewable energy solutions to position itself as a leader in sustainable mobility. By emphasizing its commitment to environmental stewardship, technological innovation, and customer satisfaction, the company aims to differentiate its brand and attract discerning consumers.

Results

Through its strategic approach informed by industry research, the company achieves significant milestones in its entry into the EV market:

- Product Launch: The company successfully launches its first electric vehicle model, garnering positive reviews from customers and industry experts for its performance, design, and sustainability features.

- Market Expansion: By leveraging its existing distribution channels and strategic partnerships, the company expands its market reach, entering new geographic markets and customer segments.

- Brand Recognition: The company's efforts to position itself as a leader in sustainable mobility yield dividends, as its brand gains recognition for its commitment to environmental responsibility and innovation.

- Revenue Growth: The company experiences accelerated revenue growth in its electric vehicle business, surpassing initial projections and contributing to overall business performance.

Lessons Learned

The case study highlights the transformative impact of industry research on strategic decision-making and business outcomes. By leveraging industry insights to inform its entry into the electric vehicle market, the company effectively navigates market dynamics, capitalizes on growth opportunities, and establishes a competitive position in the evolving mobility landscape. Key lessons learned from the case study include the importance of:

- Conducting comprehensive industry research to understand market dynamics, competitive landscapes, and consumer preferences.

- Leveraging primary and secondary research methodologies to gather qualitative and quantitative data, validate assumptions, and identify actionable insights.

- Developing a strategic roadmap aligned with market trends, customer needs, and regulatory developments to drive sustainable growth and competitive advantage.

4.3.3 Economic Indicators

In the realm of market trends analysis, economic indicators serve as crucial tools for businesses to navigate the complexities of the market landscape. These indicators provide invaluable insights into the overall health and direction of an economy, thereby influencing business strategies, investment decisions, and sales forecasting processes. Understanding economic indicators empowers organizations to anticipate changes, identify opportunities, and mitigate risks effectively.

Overview of Economic Indicators:

Economic indicators encompass a broad spectrum of metrics that reflect various aspects of economic performance, including growth, inflation, employment, consumer spending, and business activities. These indicators are categorized into leading, lagging, and coincident indicators based on their timing in relation to economic cycles.

- **Leading Indicators:** Leading indicators precede changes in economic activity and are used to forecast future trends. Examples include stock market performance, building permits, and consumer confidence indexes.

- **Lagging Indicators:** Lagging indicators, as the name suggests, trail behind changes in economic activity. These indicators confirm trends that have already occurred and are often used to validate economic forecasts. Examples include unemployment rate, corporate profits, and consumer debt levels.

- **Coincident Indicators:** Coincident indicators move in tandem with changes in economic activity, providing real-time insights into the current state of the economy. Examples include industrial production, retail sales, and GDP (Gross Domestic Product).

Importance of Economic Indicators in Market Trends Analysis:

1. Forecasting Economic Trends: Economic indicators enable businesses to forecast macroeconomic trends, such as economic growth, inflationary pressures, and consumer spending patterns. By analyzing leading indicators, organizations can anticipate shifts in the economy and adjust their strategies accordingly to capitalize on emerging opportunities or mitigate potential risks.

2. Informing Business Strategies: Economic indicators inform various aspects of business strategies, including pricing decisions, inventory management, and resource allocation. For instance, businesses may adjust their pricing strategies in response to inflationary pressures indicated by rising consumer price indexes, or they may ramp up inventory levels in anticipation of increased consumer demand signaled by improving retail sales figures.

3. Guiding Investment Decisions: Economic indicators play a pivotal role in guiding investment decisions across different asset classes, including equities, bonds, and commodities. Investors rely on indicators such as interest rates, GDP growth rates, and corporate earnings to assess the overall economic environment and identify investment opportunities with favorable risk-return profiles.

4. Assessing Market Sentiment: Economic indicators often reflect market sentiment and consumer confidence levels, which influence spending behaviors and investment sentiments. Changes in consumer confidence indexes or business sentiment surveys can signal shifts in market sentiment, impacting sales trends and investment activities.

5. Monitoring Economic Health: Economic indicators serve as barometers of economic health, providing insights into the underlying strength and resilience of an economy. By monitoring indicators such as unemployment rates, industrial production levels, and trade balances, businesses can gauge the overall health of the economy and adjust their strategies in response to changing economic conditions.

Key Economic Indicators for Market Trends Analysis:

While numerous economic indicators exist, certain key indicators are particularly relevant for businesses engaged in market trends analysis:

1. Gross Domestic Product (GDP): GDP measures the total value of goods and services produced within a country's borders and is widely regarded as a key indicator of economic performance. Changes in GDP growth rates provide insights into the pace of economic expansion or contraction, influencing consumer spending, business investment, and overall market dynamics.

2. Unemployment Rate: The unemployment rate measures the percentage of the labor force that is unemployed and actively seeking employment. Rising unemployment rates may indicate economic downturns, reducing consumer purchasing power and dampening sales prospects for businesses. Conversely, declining unemployment rates signal a tightening labor market, potentially leading to increased consumer spending and business investment.

3. Consumer Price Index (CPI): The CPI measures changes in the prices of a basket of goods and services commonly purchased by households, reflecting inflationary pressures in the economy. Businesses closely monitor CPI trends to assess the impact of rising or falling prices on consumer purchasing power and adjust their pricing strategies accordingly.

4. Interest Rates: Central banks use interest rates as a monetary policy tool to control inflation and stimulate economic activity. Changes in interest rates influence borrowing costs, investment decisions, and consumer spending patterns, thereby impacting sales trends across various industries.

5. Retail Sales: Retail sales data provide insights into consumer spending patterns and preferences, serving as a barometer of overall consumer demand. Businesses analyze retail sales figures to identify emerging trends, assess product performance, and adjust marketing strategies to capitalize on evolving consumer behaviors.

6. Business Investment: Indicators of business investment, such as capital expenditures and business confidence surveys, reflect corporate spending on equipment, technology, and infrastructure. Changes in business investment levels can signal shifts in economic sentiment and future growth prospects, influencing sales forecasts and market strategies.

7. Trade Balances: Trade balances measure the difference between a country's exports and imports of goods and services. Positive trade balances indicate net exports, contributing to economic growth and job creation, while negative trade balances may signal trade deficits and potential challenges for domestic industries.

Challenges and Limitations:

While economic indicators offer valuable insights into market trends and economic conditions, they also pose certain challenges and limitations for businesses:

1. Data Volatility and Revisions: Economic indicators are subject to revisions and data volatility, making it challenging for businesses to rely solely on current data for decision-making. Revisions to economic data can significantly impact forecasts and strategies, necessitating a flexible and adaptive approach to market analysis.

2. External Factors and Events: Economic indicators may be influenced by external factors and events beyond the control of businesses, such as geopolitical tensions, natural disasters, or global health crises. These externalities can disrupt market dynamics and complicate sales forecasting efforts, requiring businesses to incorporate risk management strategies into their planning processes.

3. Regional Variations: Economic indicators may exhibit regional variations within a country or across different global markets, reflecting localized economic conditions and consumer preferences. Businesses operating in diverse geographic regions must account for these variations in their market analysis and tailor strategies accordingly to optimize sales performance.

4. Data Interpretation Challenges: Interpreting economic indicators requires a nuanced understanding of economic theory, statistical methodologies, and market dynamics. Misinterpretation or misapplication of economic data can lead to flawed forecasts and suboptimal business decisions, highlighting the importance of rigorous analysis and expert guidance in market trends analysis.

Conclusion:

Economic indicators play a pivotal role in market trends analysis, providing businesses with valuable insights into economic conditions, consumer behaviors, and competitive dynamics. By leveraging economic indicators effectively, organizations can anticipate market trends, identify growth opportunities, and mitigate risks to enhance sales performance and achieve sustainable growth in dynamic and evolving markets.

As businesses navigate the complexities of the global economy, a comprehensive understanding of economic indicators is indispensable for informed decision-making and strategic planning. By integrating economic insights into their market analysis processes, businesses can enhance their competitive advantage, drive innovation, and adapt proactively to changing market dynamics, ultimately fueling long-term success and resilience in an ever-changing business landscape.

Illustrative Example: Impact of Interest Rate Changes on Consumer Spending

Let's consider a hypothetical scenario where a central bank decides to increase interest rates in response to inflationary pressures. This decision affects borrowing costs for consumers, businesses, and investors, subsequently influencing consumer spending patterns and overall market dynamics.

Scenario:

- Initial Conditions:

  - Current interest rate: 3%

  - Annual consumer spending: $10 million

  - Annual business investment: $5 million

  - Inflation rate: 2%

- Interest Rate Hike:

  - Central bank raises interest rates by 1% to combat inflation.

  - New interest rate: 4%

Impact on Consumer Spending:

1. Higher Borrowing Costs: With the increase in interest rates, borrowing costs for consumers rise. This leads to higher mortgage rates, increased credit card interest payments, and more expensive loans for big-ticket purchases such as cars or homes.

2. Reduced Disposable Income: Higher borrowing costs reduce consumers' disposable income as more money is allocated to debt servicing. As a result, consumers may cut back on discretionary spending, such as dining out, travel, or non-essential purchases.

3. Decreased Consumer Confidence: The prospect of higher borrowing costs and reduced purchasing power may erode consumer confidence, leading to cautious spending behaviors. Consumers may delay major purchases or opt for lower-cost alternatives, impacting sales volumes for retailers and service providers.

Quantitative Analysis:

- Projected Consumer Spending:

Initial consumer spending: $10 million

Impact of interest rate hike (hypothetical):

- Reduction in consumer spending: 10%

- New consumer spending: $9 million

- Impact on Business Investment:

The increase in interest rates may also affect business investment decisions. Higher borrowing costs can deter businesses from borrowing to finance expansion projects or capital expenditures, leading to a slowdown in investment activities.

Discussion:

In this example, the interest rate hike implemented by the central bank has tangible effects on consumer spending behavior and business investment decisions:

- **Consumer Spending:** The increase in interest rates reduces consumers' purchasing power and discretionary income, leading to a decline in consumer spending. This, in turn, can affect sales revenues for businesses across various sectors, particularly those reliant on consumer discretionary spending.

- **Business Investment:** Higher borrowing costs may deter businesses from investing in growth initiatives or capital projects, potentially leading to a contraction in business investment. Reduced investment activities can have broader implications for economic growth, job creation, and overall market sentiment.

Conclusion:

This example illustrates how changes in interest rates can influence consumer spending patterns and business investment decisions, ultimately shaping market dynamics and economic performance. By understanding the interplay between interest rates and consumer behavior, businesses can adapt their strategies to navigate changing market conditions effectively and sustain growth in an evolving economic environment.

CHAPTER V
Performance Evaluation and Optimization

5.1 Assessing Sales Team Performance

5.1.1 Individual Performance Metrics

Assessing the performance of individual sales team members is crucial for understanding their contributions to overall sales goals and identifying areas for improvement. By tracking specific metrics tailored to individual performance, sales managers can provide targeted feedback and support to help each team member reach their full potential. In this section, we will explore key individual performance metrics and how they can be effectively utilized in the evaluation process.

1. Sales Volume

Sales volume refers to the total amount of sales generated by an individual salesperson within a specific time frame, typically measured in terms of revenue or units sold. This metric provides insight into a salesperson's ability to close deals and generate revenue for the organization. By tracking sales volume over time, managers can identify trends and patterns in individual performance, as well as assess the impact of external factors such as market conditions or product changes.

2. Conversion Rate

The conversion rate measures the percentage of leads or prospects that are successfully converted into customers by an individual salesperson. It is calculated by dividing the number of closed deals by the total number of leads or prospects contacted, expressed as a percentage. A high conversion rate indicates effective selling techniques and a strong ability to persuade prospects, while a low conversion rate may signal areas for improvement in sales skills or product knowledge.

3. Average Deal Size

Average deal size refers to the average value of each sale made by an individual salesperson. This metric provides insight into the types of deals that a salesperson is closing and their ability to upsell or cross-sell additional products or services. By analyzing variations in average deal size among sales team members, managers can identify top performers who consistently close high-value deals and provide guidance to those who may benefit from strategies to increase deal size.

4. Sales Pipeline Velocity

Sales pipeline velocity measures the speed at which opportunities move through the sales pipeline, from initial contact to closing the deal. It is calculated by dividing the total value of closed deals by the average length of the sales cycle. A higher pipeline velocity indicates efficient sales processes and effective lead management, while a lower velocity may indicate bottlenecks or inefficiencies that need to be addressed. By monitoring pipeline velocity for individual sales team members, managers can identify areas where improvements can be made to accelerate the sales cycle and increase revenue.

5. Activity Metrics

Activity metrics track the number of sales-related activities performed by an individual salesperson, such as calls made, emails sent, meetings scheduled, or demos conducted.

These metrics provide insight into the level of effort and engagement exhibited by sales team members in their day-to-day activities. By setting benchmarks for activity metrics and monitoring performance against these benchmarks, managers can identify top performers who consistently meet or exceed activity targets, as well as provide support and guidance to those who may need assistance in ramping up their efforts.

6. Customer Satisfaction

Customer satisfaction measures the level of satisfaction or happiness expressed by customers who have interacted with an individual salesperson. This can be assessed through surveys, feedback forms, or direct communication with customers. High levels of customer satisfaction indicate strong relationship-building skills and a commitment to delivering excellent customer service, which are essential for building long-term customer loyalty and generating repeat business. By incorporating customer satisfaction metrics into the evaluation process, managers can identify sales team members who excel in customer interactions and recognize areas where improvement is needed to enhance the overall customer experience.

7. Revenue vs. Quota

Revenue vs. quota compares the actual revenue generated by an individual salesperson to their assigned sales quota or target. This metric provides a clear indication of whether a salesperson is meeting, exceeding, or falling short of their sales goals. By analyzing revenue vs. quota on a regular basis, managers can identify performance trends and take proactive measures to address any discrepancies. For example, if a salesperson consistently fails to meet their quota, additional training or support may be necessary to help them improve their performance and achieve their targets.

Conclusion

In conclusion, assessing individual sales team performance requires a comprehensive approach that incorporates a variety of metrics tailored to the specific roles and responsibilities of each salesperson. By tracking key performance indicators such as sales volume, conversion rate, average deal size, sales pipeline velocity, activity metrics, customer satisfaction, and revenue vs. quota, managers can gain valuable insights into the strengths and weaknesses of their sales team members and take proactive steps to optimize performance and drive growth. Effective performance evaluation and feedback mechanisms are essential for fostering a culture of continuous improvement and empowering sales professionals to achieve their full potential.

5.1.2 Team Performance Metrics

Assessing the performance of a sales team is a critical aspect of sales management. While individual performance metrics provide insights into the capabilities and contributions of each salesperson, team performance metrics offer a broader perspective on how well the team is functioning as a cohesive unit to achieve its goals. By tracking and analyzing team performance metrics, sales managers can identify strengths and weaknesses within the team dynamics, pinpoint areas for improvement, and implement strategies to enhance overall effectiveness. In this section, we delve into key team performance metrics that sales managers should consider when evaluating the performance of their sales teams.

1. Sales Target Achievement

One of the fundamental metrics for assessing team performance is the extent to which the team meets its sales targets. This metric provides a clear indication of the team's overall effectiveness in generating revenue and driving business growth. Sales targets may be set for specific time periods, such as monthly, quarterly, or annually, and can be based on revenue, units sold, or other relevant metrics. By comparing actual sales performance against the targets, sales managers can evaluate the team's success in meeting predefined objectives.

2. Sales Pipeline Health

The health of the sales pipeline is another important indicator of team performance. The sales pipeline represents the series of stages that leads and prospects move through as they progress towards making a purchase. Monitoring key metrics such as the number of leads, conversion rates at each stage, average deal size, and sales velocity provides insights into the efficiency and effectiveness of the team's sales process. A healthy pipeline with a steady flow of qualified leads and a high conversion rate indicates that the team is effectively engaging with prospects and moving them towards closure.

3. Customer Satisfaction

Customer satisfaction is a critical metric that reflects the team's ability to meet the needs and expectations of its customers. Happy and satisfied customers are more likely to make repeat purchases, provide positive referrals, and contribute to the overall success of the business. Sales managers can measure customer satisfaction through various means, such as surveys, feedback forms, or Net Promoter Score (NPS) ratings. By regularly monitoring customer satisfaction metrics, sales managers can identify areas where improvements are needed and take proactive steps to enhance the customer experience.

4. Sales Team Collaboration

Effective collaboration among team members is essential for achieving collective goals and driving success in sales. Metrics related to team collaboration, such as communication frequency, cross-selling opportunities, and knowledge sharing, can provide insights into the level of synergy and cohesion within the team. Sales managers can track these metrics using collaboration tools, CRM systems, or regular team meetings. By fostering a culture of collaboration and teamwork, sales managers can leverage the collective strengths of the team to maximize performance and achieve greater results.

5. Sales Efficiency and Productivity

Sales efficiency and productivity metrics measure the team's ability to generate revenue while minimizing the time and resources required to do so. Key metrics in this category may include sales per rep, sales cycle length, win rate, and activity levels (such as calls made, emails sent, and meetings held). By analyzing these metrics, sales managers can identify opportunities to streamline processes, eliminate bottlenecks, and optimize resource allocation to improve overall efficiency and productivity.

6. Sales Forecast Accuracy

Accurate sales forecasting is essential for effective resource planning, budgeting, and decision-making within an organization. Sales managers can assess the team's forecasting accuracy by comparing predicted sales figures with actual results over time. Metrics such as forecast variance, forecasting bias, and forecasted-to-actual ratios provide insights into the reliability and precision of the team's sales forecasts. By improving forecasting accuracy, sales managers can enhance the organization's ability to anticipate market trends, allocate resources effectively, and capitalize on growth opportunities.

7. Employee Engagement and Retention

Employee engagement and retention are critical factors that directly impact team performance and overall organizational success. High levels of engagement contribute to increased motivation, productivity, and job satisfaction among team members, leading to better performance outcomes. Sales managers can measure employee engagement through metrics such as employee satisfaction surveys, retention rates, and turnover rates. By prioritizing employee engagement and implementing strategies to support the well-being and professional development of team members, sales managers can foster a positive work environment conducive to high performance and long-term retention.

Conclusion

In conclusion, assessing team performance is essential for optimizing the effectiveness and efficiency of a sales team. By monitoring and analyzing key team performance metrics, sales managers can gain valuable insights into the strengths and weaknesses of the team, identify areas for improvement, and implement strategies to enhance overall performance. From sales target achievement and pipeline health to customer satisfaction and employee engagement, a comprehensive approach to evaluating team performance enables sales managers to drive growth, maximize revenue, and achieve sustainable success in today's competitive business landscape.

5.1.3 Performance Reviews and Feedback

Performance reviews and feedback play a pivotal role in the continuous improvement of sales team performance. They serve as a mechanism for assessing individual and team accomplishments, identifying areas for development, and fostering a culture of accountability and growth within the organization. In this section, we delve into the intricacies of conducting effective performance reviews and providing constructive feedback.

Importance of Performance Reviews

Performance reviews serve multiple purposes within an organization. They provide an opportunity for managers to communicate expectations clearly, evaluate employees' progress towards goals, recognize achievements, and address any concerns or areas needing improvement. Additionally, performance reviews serve as a platform for employees to voice their own perspectives, seek guidance on career development, and align their objectives with those of the organization.

Regular performance reviews contribute to employee engagement and motivation by demonstrating that their contributions are valued and recognized. They also facilitate open communication between managers and team members, fostering trust and transparency within the organization. By identifying strengths and weaknesses, performance reviews enable targeted training and development initiatives to enhance overall team effectiveness.

Components of Performance Reviews

Effective performance reviews incorporate a comprehensive evaluation of various aspects of an employee's performance, including but not limited to:

1. Goal Achievement: Assessing the extent to which employees have met their performance objectives and key performance indicators (KPIs). This involves reviewing sales targets, quotas, and other relevant metrics established at the beginning of the performance period.

2. Sales Metrics: Analyzing quantitative data related to sales performance, such as revenue generated, number of deals closed, conversion rates, pipeline velocity, and average deal size. These metrics provide insights into individual sales productivity and effectiveness.

3. Customer Feedback: Soliciting feedback from customers or clients regarding their interactions with the sales team member. This could involve conducting customer satisfaction surveys, collecting testimonials, or reviewing customer complaints and compliments.

4. Competency Assessment: Evaluating the sales skills, knowledge, and competencies demonstrated by the employee in various aspects of the sales process, including prospecting, lead qualification, negotiation, and closing.

5. Behavioral Evaluation: Assessing the employee's behavior, attitude, and professionalism in dealing with colleagues, superiors, and clients. This includes communication skills, teamwork, adaptability, and adherence to company values and policies.

6. Self-Assessment: Encouraging employees to reflect on their own performance, strengths, areas for improvement, and professional development goals. Self-assessment can provide valuable insights into employees' perceptions of their performance and career aspirations.

Conducting Performance Reviews

Effective performance reviews require careful planning, preparation, and execution to ensure meaningful and constructive feedback. Here are some best practices for conducting performance reviews:

1. Establish Clear Objectives: Define the purpose and objectives of the performance review, including what specific aspects of performance will be evaluated and discussed.

2. Schedule Regular Reviews: Conduct performance reviews at regular intervals, such as quarterly or annually, to provide consistent feedback and track progress over time.

3. Prepare Documentation: Gather relevant data, metrics, and documentation to support the evaluation of performance, including sales reports, customer feedback, and performance appraisals.

4. Create a Positive Atmosphere: Set a positive and supportive tone for the performance review meeting, emphasizing the importance of growth, development, and mutual respect.

5. Provide Specific Feedback: Offer specific examples and evidence to support feedback, focusing on behaviors, outcomes, and areas for improvement rather than personal characteristics.

6. Encourage Two-Way Communication: Foster open dialogue during the performance review, allowing employees to share their perspectives, challenges, and aspirations.

7. Set SMART Goals: Collaboratively establish clear, measurable, achievable, relevant, and time-bound (SMART) goals for future performance improvement and development.

8. Offer Support and Resources: Identify training, coaching, or support resources available to help employees address areas for improvement and achieve their goals.

9. Document Action Plans: Document key takeaways, action items, and commitments made during the performance review meeting, and follow up regularly to monitor progress.

Providing Constructive Feedback

Constructive feedback is an essential component of performance reviews, enabling employees to learn and grow professionally. When providing feedback, it is important to focus on specific behaviors or outcomes, be objective and non-judgmental, and offer actionable suggestions for improvement. Here are some guidelines for providing constructive feedback:

1. Be Timely: Provide feedback in a timely manner, ideally as close to the observed behavior or performance as possible. This allows employees to address issues promptly and make necessary adjustments.

2. Be Specific: Focus on specific behaviors, actions, or outcomes rather than making generalizations or personal criticisms. Provide concrete examples or evidence to support your feedback.

3. Use the "Feedback Sandwich" Approach: Start with positive feedback or acknowledgment of strengths, then address areas for improvement, and conclude with encouragement or support. This approach helps balance constructive criticism with positive reinforcement.

4. Be Objective: Base feedback on observable facts and evidence rather than personal opinions or assumptions. Avoid making judgments or attributing motives to the individual.

5. Focus on Improvement: Frame feedback as an opportunity for growth and development rather than punishment or reprimand. Emphasize how addressing areas for improvement can help the employee achieve their goals and enhance their performance.

6. Invite Dialogue: Encourage employees to ask questions, seek clarification, or share their perspective on the feedback provided. Foster a two-way dialogue to ensure mutual understanding and alignment.

7. Offer Support: Identify resources, tools, or support mechanisms available to help employees address areas for improvement, such as training programs, coaching, or mentoring.

8. Follow Up: Schedule follow-up discussions to review progress, provide ongoing support and feedback, and adjust goals or action plans as needed.

Conclusion

Performance reviews and feedback are essential tools for assessing sales team performance, identifying areas for improvement, and fostering a culture of continuous learning and development. By conducting regular performance reviews and providing constructive feedback, organizations can empower their sales teams to achieve their full potential, drive revenue growth, and deliver exceptional customer experiences. Effective performance management requires a strategic approach, clear communication, and a commitment to ongoing improvement at both the individual and organizational levels.

5.2 Identifying Areas for Improvement

In any business endeavor, the quest for improvement is perpetual. Identifying areas that require enhancement is fundamental for sustained growth and competitiveness. One of the most effective methods for this task is conducting a gap analysis. Gap analysis is a systematic approach that compares current performance with desired outcomes, revealing the gaps between the two. By pinpointing these gaps, organizations can strategize and allocate resources more effectively to achieve their goals. In this section, we delve into the intricacies of conducting a gap analysis and how it can be utilized as a powerful tool for improvement.

5.2.1 Gap Analysis

Gap analysis is a strategic management tool used to assess the disparity between an organization's current performance and its desired state. It involves identifying the gaps in performance, processes, resources, and capabilities that hinder the attainment of objectives. By recognizing these gaps, businesses can develop targeted action plans to bridge them, thereby aligning their operations with their strategic goals.

Understanding the Process of Gap Analysis

The process of conducting a gap analysis typically involves several key steps:

1. Defining Objectives: The first step is to clearly define the objectives or goals that the organization aims to achieve. These objectives should be specific, measurable, achievable, relevant, and time-bound (SMART).

2. Assessing Current Performance: Once the objectives are established, the next step is to evaluate the organization's current performance in relation to these goals. This assessment involves gathering relevant data and metrics to measure performance across various areas such as sales, marketing, operations, customer service, etc.

3. Identifying Performance Gaps: After assessing current performance, the gaps between the actual and desired outcomes are identified. These gaps could exist in terms of sales targets, market share, customer satisfaction levels, operational efficiency, or any other relevant metrics.

4. Analyzing Causes of Gaps: Once the gaps are identified, the next step is to analyze the underlying causes contributing to these discrepancies. This analysis may involve examining factors such as inadequate resources, inefficient processes, lack of skills or training, technological limitations, competitive pressures, etc.

5. Developing Action Plans: Based on the analysis of performance gaps and their causes, action plans are formulated to address these issues. These plans outline specific steps, timelines, responsibilities, and resources required to bridge the gaps and improve performance.

6. Implementing and Monitoring Progress: The final step involves implementing the action plans and closely monitoring their progress. Regular performance monitoring and review are essential to ensure that the corrective measures are effective and yielding the desired results.

Types of Gap Analysis

Gap analysis can be categorized into several types, each serving different purposes and focusing on specific areas of improvement:

1. Performance Gap Analysis: This type of analysis focuses on identifying discrepancies between actual performance and desired performance levels. It helps organizations pinpoint areas where performance improvement is needed to achieve strategic objectives.

2. Market Gap Analysis: Market gap analysis assesses the disparity between current market demand and the organization's market share or product offerings. It helps businesses identify opportunities for expansion or diversification to capture untapped market potential.

3. Skills Gap Analysis: Skills gap analysis evaluates the disparity between the skills and competencies required for various roles within the organization and the skills possessed by employees. It aids in identifying training needs and developing talent management strategies.

4. Technology Gap Analysis: Technology gap analysis examines the misalignment between current technological capabilities and the technology requirements to support business objectives. It guides organizations in selecting and implementing appropriate technologies to enhance operational efficiency and innovation.

5. Resource Gap Analysis: Resource gap analysis assesses the inadequacy or misallocation of resources such as finances, manpower, infrastructure, etc., needed to achieve organizational goals. It helps in optimizing resource utilization and planning for future resource allocation.

Benefits of Gap Analysis

Conducting a thorough gap analysis offers several benefits for organizations:

1. Strategic Alignment: Gap analysis aligns organizational activities and resources with strategic objectives, ensuring that efforts are directed towards achieving desired outcomes.

2. Prioritization of Efforts: By identifying areas with the greatest performance gaps, organizations can prioritize their improvement efforts and allocate resources more effectively.

3. Informed Decision-Making: Gap analysis provides valuable insights into the root causes of performance discrepancies, enabling informed decision-making on corrective actions and resource allocation.

4. Continuous Improvement: Gap analysis fosters a culture of continuous improvement within the organization by systematically identifying and addressing areas for enhancement.

5. Competitive Advantage: By bridging performance gaps and improving efficiency, organizations can gain a competitive edge in the marketplace, driving growth and profitability.

Challenges and Considerations

While gap analysis offers numerous benefits, it is not without its challenges and considerations:

1. Data Availability and Accuracy: Conducting a gap analysis requires access to reliable data and metrics. Ensuring the availability and accuracy of data can be challenging, particularly in complex organizational environments.

2. Subjectivity and Bias: The interpretation of performance data and the identification of gaps may be influenced by subjective judgments and biases. It is essential to maintain objectivity and involve multiple stakeholders in the analysis process.

3. Complexity of Analysis: Analyzing the root causes of performance gaps and developing effective action plans can be complex and time-consuming. It requires interdisciplinary collaboration and expertise to address multifaceted issues comprehensively.

4. Resistance to Change: Implementing corrective actions to bridge performance gaps may face resistance from stakeholders who are reluctant to change established processes or practices. Effective change management strategies are essential to overcome resistance and foster organizational buy-in.

5. Dynamic Business Environment: The business landscape is constantly evolving, with market dynamics, technological advancements, and competitive pressures influencing organizational performance. Gap analysis needs to be regularly reviewed and updated to remain relevant in a dynamic environment.

Case Study: Implementing Gap Analysis in Sales Performance

To illustrate the practical application of gap analysis, let us consider a case study of a software company seeking to improve its sales performance. The company sets a strategic objective to increase its annual sales revenue by 20% within the next fiscal year. However, upon conducting a gap analysis, it identifies several key areas where performance falls short of this target:

1. Sales Team Productivity: The analysis reveals that the average sales productivity per representative is below industry benchmarks. Factors contributing to this gap include inadequate sales training, limited access to sales enablement tools, and inefficient lead management processes.

2. Customer Acquisition Rate: The company's customer acquisition rate is lower than desired, indicating challenges in converting leads into paying customers. Issues such as ineffective sales prospecting strategies, insufficient market segmentation, and suboptimal sales messaging contribute to this performance gap.

3. Sales Cycle Length: The analysis identifies an extended sales cycle length, resulting in delayed revenue realization and increased customer acquisition costs. Root causes of this gap include poor qualification of leads, lack of sales automation tools, and ineffective sales pipeline management.

Based on these findings, the company develops a comprehensive action plan to address the identified performance gaps:

1. Sales Training and Development: Implement targeted sales training programs to enhance the skills and competencies of the sales team, focusing on areas such as prospecting, negotiation, and objection handling.

2. Sales Enablement Tools: Invest in sales enablement tools and technology platforms to streamline the sales process, improve lead management, and provide sales representatives with access to relevant resources and content.

3. Lead Qualification and Segmentation: Refine lead qualification criteria and segmentation strategies to prioritize high-potential prospects and tailor sales approaches accordingly. Implement lead scoring methodologies to identify qualified leads more efficiently.

4. Sales Process Optimization: Review and optimize the sales process to reduce friction points, streamline workflows, and accelerate deal closure. Leverage automation tools for tasks such as email outreach, proposal generation, and contract management.

5. Performance Monitoring and Feedback: Establish regular performance monitoring mechanisms to track progress against sales targets and provide timely feedback to sales representatives. Implement performance dashboards and KPI tracking systems to facilitate transparency and accountability.

By implementing these targeted interventions based on the findings of the gap analysis, the company successfully improves its sales performance and achieves its revenue growth targets within the specified timeframe. The systematic approach to identifying and addressing performance gaps enables the organization to optimize its sales operations and drive sustainable business growth.

Conclusion

Gap analysis is a powerful tool for identifying areas of improvement and aligning organizational efforts with strategic objectives. By systematically assessing performance gaps, analyzing root causes, and developing targeted action plans, businesses can enhance their competitive position, drive operational efficiency, and achieve sustainable growth. However, conducting a gap analysis requires careful planning, data-driven analysis, and effective implementation to realize its full potential. With a commitment to continuous improvement and a strategic focus on bridging performance gaps, organizations can navigate challenges, capitalize on opportunities, and thrive in today's dynamic business environment.

5.2.2 Root Cause Analysis

Root Cause Analysis (RCA) is a systematic process for identifying the underlying causes of problems or issues within an organization. It's a vital component of performance evaluation and optimization because it helps to pinpoint the fundamental reasons behind any shortcomings or inefficiencies in sales processes. By addressing root causes rather than symptoms, businesses can implement more effective solutions and drive sustainable improvements in sales performance.

Understanding Root Cause Analysis

Root Cause Analysis operates on the principle that every problem has a specific set of underlying causes. These causes, when addressed, can prevent the recurrence of the problem. RCA involves a structured approach to identifying these root causes by examining the sequence of events leading up to the issue. It's essential to distinguish between immediate causes (symptoms) and root causes to ensure that corrective actions target the source of the problem.

Steps in Root Cause Analysis

1. Define the Problem:

Clearly articulate the issue or problem that requires analysis. This step ensures that everyone involved understands the scope and nature of the problem.

2. Collect Data:

Gather relevant data and information related to the problem. This may include sales metrics, customer feedback, process documentation, and any other relevant sources of information.

3. Identify Possible Causes:

Brainstorm potential factors or events that may have contributed to the problem. This step involves considering various perspectives and exploring different avenues that could lead to the identified issue.

4. Narrow Down Causes:

Evaluate the list of potential causes and prioritize them based on their likelihood and impact. This step may involve conducting further analysis or investigation to gather more insights into each potential cause.

5. Determine Root Cause(s):

Once the list of potential causes is narrowed down, delve deeper into each one to identify the root cause(s). The root cause is the underlying reason or factor that, if addressed, could prevent the problem from occurring again.

6. Develop Solutions:

Based on the identified root cause(s), brainstorm and develop potential solutions or corrective actions. These solutions should directly address the root cause(s) to effectively resolve the problem.

7. Implement Solutions:

Put the selected solutions into action. Ensure clear communication and coordination among relevant stakeholders to facilitate smooth implementation.

8. Monitor and Evaluate:

Continuously monitor the effectiveness of the implemented solutions. Evaluate whether the problem has been resolved or mitigated and make adjustments as necessary.

Tools and Techniques for Root Cause Analysis

Several tools and techniques can aid in conducting Root Cause Analysis effectively. Some commonly used ones include:

Fishbone Diagram (Ishikawa Diagram):

This visual tool helps identify potential causes of a problem by categorizing them into various branches, such as people, process, equipment, materials, and environment.

5 Whys Technique:

This technique involves repeatedly asking "why" to drill down to the underlying cause of a problem. By asking "why" multiple times, teams can uncover deeper layers of causality.

Pareto Analysis:

Pareto Analysis, also known as the 80/20 rule, helps prioritize potential causes by focusing on the most significant contributors to the problem.

Failure Mode and Effects Analysis (FMEA):

FMEA is a systematic approach to identifying and preventing potential failures in processes, products, or systems. It helps prioritize risks based on their severity, occurrence probability, and detectability.

Challenges and Considerations

While Root Cause Analysis can be a powerful tool for improving sales performance, it's essential to acknowledge some challenges and considerations:

Data Availability and Quality:

RCA relies heavily on accurate and comprehensive data. Ensuring access to relevant data sources and maintaining data quality is crucial for the effectiveness of the analysis.

Subjectivity and Bias:

The process of identifying root causes may be influenced by personal biases or organizational politics. It's essential to foster an environment of openness and objectivity to overcome these biases.

Time and Resource Constraints:

Conducting a thorough Root Cause Analysis can be time-consuming and resource-intensive. Organizations must allocate adequate time and resources to ensure a comprehensive analysis.

Complexity of Interactions:

Sales processes are often complex, involving various stakeholders and interactions. Understanding the interdependencies between different factors can be challenging but is essential for accurate root cause identification.

Case Study: Applying Root Cause Analysis in Sales Optimization

Let's consider a hypothetical case study to illustrate how Root Cause Analysis can be applied in a sales context:

Case Study: Declining Sales Performance

Problem Statement: A company has experienced a significant decline in sales performance over the past quarter, despite consistent efforts to boost sales.

Root Cause Analysis:

1. Define the Problem: The problem is the decline in sales performance.

2. Collect Data: Gather sales data, customer feedback, and performance metrics from the past quarter.

3. Identify Possible Causes: Potential causes may include changes in market conditions, competitive pressures, ineffective sales strategies, or issues with product quality.

4. Narrow Down Causes: Based on initial analysis, focus on factors related to sales strategies and customer engagement.

5. Determine Root Cause(s):

   - After analyzing sales data and conducting interviews with sales team members, it becomes evident that recent changes in the sales process, including a shift in target demographics and modifications to the sales pitch, have led to confusion and decreased effectiveness.

   - Additionally, inadequate training and support for sales representatives in adapting to these changes have exacerbated the problem.

6. Develop Solutions:

   - Revise the sales strategy to better align with the target demographics and market trends.

   - Provide additional training and resources for sales representatives to improve their understanding and execution of the new sales process.

7. Implement Solutions: Roll out the revised sales strategy and initiate training programs for sales teams.

8. Monitor and Evaluate: Continuously track sales performance metrics and gather feedback from sales representatives and customers to assess the impact of the implemented solutions. Make adjustments as necessary to ensure sustained improvement.

Conclusion

Root Cause Analysis is a valuable tool for identifying and addressing the underlying factors contributing to sales performance issues. By systematically examining the root causes of problems, organizations can implement targeted solutions that drive meaningful improvements in sales effectiveness and efficiency. However, conducting RCA requires careful planning, access to relevant data, and a commitment to objectivity and thorough analysis. When applied effectively, RCA can help organizations optimize their sales processes, enhance customer satisfaction, and achieve sustainable growth.

5.2.3 SWOT Analysis

SWOT analysis is a strategic planning tool used to evaluate the Strengths, Weaknesses, Opportunities, and Threats involved in a business venture or project. It can be applied at various levels within an organization, from individual departments to the entire company. In the context of sales metrics and analytics, conducting a SWOT analysis can provide valuable insights into areas for improvement and potential avenues for growth. This section explores how SWOT analysis can be effectively utilized within the sales function.

Strengths:

Strengths refer to the internal attributes and resources that give an organization an advantage over others in the market. When conducting a SWOT analysis for sales performance, identifying and leveraging strengths can help capitalize on existing opportunities and mitigate potential threats. Some examples of strengths in the context of sales include:

1. Established brand reputation: A strong brand presence can facilitate easier sales conversions and instill confidence in potential customers.

2. High-quality products or services: Offering superior products or services compared to competitors can be a significant strength, attracting customers and fostering loyalty.

3. Experienced sales team: A skilled and knowledgeable sales team can effectively communicate value propositions and address customer needs, leading to higher sales volumes.

4. Efficient sales processes: Streamlined sales processes, supported by effective CRM systems and tools, can enhance productivity and maximize sales efficiency.

Weaknesses:

Weaknesses are internal factors that may hinder an organization's ability to achieve its objectives or compete effectively in the market. Identifying weaknesses is crucial for developing strategies to overcome challenges and improve performance. In the context of sales, some common weaknesses may include:

1. Limited product range: A narrow product or service offering may restrict sales opportunities and limit market penetration.

2. Inadequate training and development: Insufficient training programs or lack of ongoing skill development can result in underperforming sales teams and missed sales targets.

3. Poor customer service: Subpar customer support or ineffective handling of customer inquiries and complaints can lead to lost sales and damaged reputation.

4. Inefficient lead generation: Ineffective lead generation strategies or outdated prospecting techniques can result in wasted resources and missed sales opportunities.

Opportunities:

Opportunities are external factors or market conditions that an organization could exploit to its advantage. Identifying opportunities allows businesses to capitalize on emerging trends and gain a competitive edge. In the context of sales, some potential opportunities may include:

1. Market expansion: Entering new geographic markets or targeting different customer segments can unlock new revenue streams and drive business growth.

2. Technological advancements: Embracing innovative sales technologies, such as AI-driven analytics or virtual sales platforms, can enhance sales effectiveness and efficiency.

3. Strategic partnerships: Collaborating with complementary businesses or forming alliances with industry leaders can broaden market reach and increase sales opportunities.

4. Changing consumer preferences: Anticipating and adapting to shifts in consumer behavior or preferences can enable businesses to tailor their offerings and better meet customer needs.

Threats:

Threats are external factors or challenges that have the potential to negatively impact an organization's performance or competitive position. Identifying threats allows businesses to proactively mitigate risks and safeguard against potential pitfalls. In the context of sales, some common threats may include:

1. Intense competition: Competitors entering the market or existing rivals launching aggressive marketing campaigns can pose a threat to sales revenue and market share.

2. Economic downturns: Economic instability or recessions can lead to reduced consumer spending and a slowdown in sales growth.

3. Regulatory changes: Changes in government regulations or industry standards can introduce compliance challenges and increase operational costs for businesses.

4. Technological disruption: Rapid advancements in technology or shifts in consumer preferences towards online purchasing can disrupt traditional sales channels and business models.

Conclusion:

SWOT analysis is a valuable tool for assessing the internal strengths and weaknesses of a sales organization, as well as identifying external opportunities and threats in the market environment. By conducting a thorough SWOT analysis, sales leaders can gain valuable insights into areas for improvement and develop strategies to optimize sales performance and drive sustainable growth. Additionally, SWOT analysis can help sales teams adapt to changing market conditions, mitigate risks, and capitalize on emerging opportunities, thereby maintaining a competitive advantage in the marketplace.

5.3 Strategies for Optimization

5.3.1 Training and Development Programs

Training and development programs are essential components of optimizing sales performance within any organization. These initiatives not only enhance the skills and knowledge of sales teams but also foster a culture of continuous improvement. In this section, we'll delve into various aspects of designing, implementing, and evaluating effective training and development programs tailored for sales teams.

Designing Effective Training Programs:

Designing an effective training program involves careful consideration of various factors, including the specific needs of the sales team, organizational objectives, and available resources. Here are key steps to designing impactful training programs:

1. Needs Assessment: Conduct a thorough assessment to identify the knowledge and skill gaps within the sales team. This can be done through surveys, interviews, performance evaluations, and feedback from sales managers.

2. Setting Objectives: Clearly define the objectives of the training program based on the identified needs. Objectives should be specific, measurable, achievable, relevant, and time-bound (SMART).

3. Content Development: Develop training content that aligns with the identified objectives. This may include product knowledge, sales techniques, negotiation skills, customer relationship management, and use of sales tools and technologies.

4. Delivery Methods: Choose appropriate delivery methods based on the content and learning preferences of the sales team. This may include classroom training, online courses, workshops, role-playing exercises, on-the-job training, and mentoring/coaching.

5. Engagement and Interactivity: Incorporate interactive elements such as case studies, simulations, group discussions, and hands-on activities to keep participants engaged and facilitate better learning retention.

6. Feedback Mechanisms: Implement mechanisms for collecting feedback from participants to evaluate the effectiveness of the training program and identify areas for improvement.

Implementing Training Programs:

Once the training program is designed, the next step is its implementation. Effective implementation ensures that training objectives are met and that participants are actively engaged throughout the process. Here are some best practices for implementing training programs:

1. Communication and Promotion: Clearly communicate the details of the training program, including objectives, schedule, and expectations, to all relevant stakeholders. Promote the program as an opportunity for professional development and growth.

2. Resource Allocation: Allocate necessary resources, including budget, time, and personnel, for the successful implementation of the training program. Ensure that trainers/instructors are well-prepared and equipped to deliver the content effectively.

3. Logistics and Support: Take care of logistical arrangements such as venue booking, equipment setup, and provision of training materials. Provide adequate support to participants, including access to resources and assistance with any technical issues.

4. Engagement Strategies: Implement strategies to maintain participant engagement throughout the training program. This may include incorporating interactive elements, encouraging active participation, and addressing questions and concerns in real-time.

5. Monitoring and Evaluation: Monitor the progress of the training program to ensure that it is on track and meeting its objectives. Collect feedback from participants and trainers/instructors to identify any issues or areas for improvement.

6. Adaptation and Flexibility: Be flexible and adaptable in response to any unexpected challenges or changes in circumstances. Modify the training program as needed to address emerging needs or issues.

Evaluating Training Effectiveness:

Evaluation is crucial for assessing the impact of training programs and identifying areas for improvement. Various methods can be used to evaluate the effectiveness of sales training programs:

1. Pre and Post-Assessments: Conduct assessments before and after the training program to measure changes in knowledge, skills, and attitudes among participants.

2. Performance Metrics: Track relevant performance metrics, such as sales revenue, conversion rates, customer satisfaction scores, and sales team productivity, before and after the training program.

3. Participant Feedback: Gather feedback from participants through surveys, interviews, or focus groups to gauge their satisfaction with the training program and gather insights into areas for improvement.

4. Manager Feedback: Solicit feedback from sales managers and supervisors to assess the impact of the training program on sales team performance and identify any observed improvements or challenges.

5. ROI Analysis: Conduct a return on investment (ROI) analysis to evaluate the financial impact of the training program by comparing the costs incurred with the benefits gained, such as increased sales revenue or cost savings.

6. Long-Term Monitoring: Continuously monitor the long-term effects of the training program on sales performance and business outcomes to determine its sustained impact over time.

Conclusion:

Effective training and development programs are critical for optimizing sales performance and driving business growth. By identifying training needs, designing tailored programs, implementing them effectively, and evaluating their impact, organizations can empower their sales teams with the knowledge, skills, and tools they need to succeed in today's competitive marketplace. Investing in ongoing training and development not only benefits individual sales representatives but also contributes to the overall success and profitability of the organization.

5.3.2 Process Improvement Initiatives

Process improvement initiatives are integral to enhancing the efficiency and effectiveness of sales operations. By systematically reviewing and refining existing processes, organizations can streamline workflows, reduce costs, and ultimately drive higher sales performance. This section explores various strategies and methodologies for implementing process improvement initiatives within a sales environment.

Lean Methodology

Lean methodology, originating from Toyota's manufacturing processes, focuses on minimizing waste while maximizing value. Applied to sales, lean principles aim to eliminate non-value-added activities and optimize resource utilization. Key components of lean methodology in sales include:

Value Stream Mapping (VSM): VSM involves visualizing the end-to-end sales process to identify areas of inefficiency and waste. By mapping out every step from lead generation to conversion, organizations can pinpoint bottlenecks and opportunities for improvement.

Kaizen Events: Kaizen, meaning continuous improvement in Japanese, refers to short-term, focused initiatives aimed at addressing specific issues within the sales process. These events bring together cross-functional teams to brainstorm solutions, test hypotheses, and implement changes rapidly.

Just-in-Time (JIT) Delivery: JIT delivery entails supplying resources, information, and support precisely when they are needed in the sales process, minimizing inventory and reducing delays. This approach enhances agility and responsiveness, enabling sales teams to adapt quickly to changing customer demands.

Six Sigma

Six Sigma is a data-driven methodology focused on reducing defects and variations in processes to achieve consistent, high-quality outcomes. While originally developed for manufacturing, Six Sigma principles can be applied to sales processes to enhance precision and reliability. Key elements of Six Sigma in sales include:

Define, Measure, Analyze, Improve, Control (DMAIC): DMAIC is a structured problem-solving approach used to identify and rectify issues within the sales process. This methodology involves defining project goals, measuring current performance, analyzing root causes of problems, implementing improvements, and establishing controls to sustain results.

Statistical Process Control (SPC): SPC involves monitoring and controlling variations in sales processes using statistical techniques. By collecting and analyzing data in real-time, organizations can identify trends, detect deviations from desired performance levels, and take corrective action proactively.

Voice of the Customer (VOC) Analysis: VOC analysis involves capturing customer feedback and preferences to inform process improvements. By understanding the needs and expectations of customers, organizations can align their sales processes more closely with customer requirements, enhancing satisfaction and loyalty.

Agile Methodology

Agile methodology, originally developed for software development, emphasizes iterative, incremental approaches to project management. Applied to sales, agile principles enable teams to adapt quickly to market changes and customer feedback. Key components of agile methodology in sales include:

Scrum Framework: Scrum is a popular agile framework that divides work into short, time-boxed iterations called sprints. Sales teams using scrum hold regular meetings, or "stand-ups," to review progress, identify obstacles, and adjust priorities accordingly.

Kanban Boards: Kanban is a visual project management tool that helps teams visualize workflow and prioritize tasks. Sales teams can use Kanban boards to track leads, opportunities, and deals through various stages of the sales pipeline, facilitating transparency and collaboration.

Cross-Functional Collaboration: Agile encourages collaboration between sales, marketing, product development, and other departments to ensure alignment and synergy across the organization. By breaking down silos and fostering communication, agile methodologies can improve responsiveness and agility in sales operations.

Total Quality Management (TQM)

Total Quality Management (TQM) is a holistic approach to quality management that involves continuous improvement, customer focus, and employee empowerment. In the context of sales, TQM principles emphasize the importance of delivering value to customers while striving for excellence in every aspect of the sales process. Key tenets of TQM in sales include:

Continuous Improvement: TQM advocates for ongoing refinement of sales processes, products, and services to meet or exceed customer expectations. By fostering a culture of continuous improvement, organizations can drive innovation and maintain a competitive edge in the marketplace.

Customer Focus: TQM places a strong emphasis on understanding and satisfying customer needs and preferences. Sales teams adopting a customer-centric approach seek to build long-term relationships based on trust, integrity, and mutual value creation.

Employee Empowerment: TQM recognizes the critical role of employees in delivering quality outcomes. By empowering sales professionals with the autonomy, resources, and support they need to excel, organizations can foster a sense of ownership and accountability, driving higher levels of performance and engagement.

Conclusion

Process improvement initiatives are essential for optimizing sales performance and driving sustainable growth. By leveraging methodologies such as lean, Six Sigma, agile, and TQM, organizations can streamline workflows, enhance quality, and align sales processes more closely with customer needs and market dynamics. However, successful implementation requires strong leadership, cross-functional collaboration, and a commitment to continuous improvement throughout the organization. By embracing a culture of innovation and excellence, sales teams can achieve greater efficiency, effectiveness, and ultimately, superior results in today's competitive business landscape.

5.3.3 Incentive Structures

Incentive structures are vital components of sales management, designed to motivate and reward sales teams for achieving specific targets and objectives. Crafting effective incentive structures requires a deep understanding of the organization's goals, sales processes, and the dynamics of the sales team. This section explores various incentive structures commonly employed in sales management and discusses best practices for their implementation.

Understanding Incentive Structures

Incentive structures can take various forms, including monetary rewards, recognition, career advancement opportunities, and non-monetary benefits. The key is to align incentives with desired behaviors and outcomes while ensuring fairness and transparency. Before designing an incentive structure, it's essential to identify the objectives it aims to achieve. These objectives may include increasing sales volume, promoting specific products or services, expanding into new markets, or enhancing customer satisfaction and loyalty.

Types of Incentive Structures

1. Commission-Based Incentives

Commission-based incentives are among the most traditional and widely used structures in sales management. Sales representatives earn a percentage of the revenue generated from their sales. This structure directly ties compensation to performance, providing a clear incentive for driving sales. However, it's crucial to establish fair commission rates that motivate salespeople without excessively burdening the organization's expenses.

2. Performance Bonuses

Performance bonuses are one-time or periodic rewards given to sales professionals for achieving predetermined targets or milestones. These targets may be based on sales volume, revenue, customer acquisition, or other key performance indicators (KPIs). Performance bonuses can serve as powerful motivators, especially when they are challenging yet attainable. They also provide an opportunity to recognize and reward exceptional performance within the sales team.

3. Sales Contests and Challenges

Sales contests and challenges introduce an element of competition among sales team members by setting specific goals and offering rewards to top performers. These initiatives can be short-term or ongoing, focusing on various aspects of the sales process, such as prospecting, closing deals, or upselling. Sales contests not only incentivize individual performance but also foster a sense of camaraderie and teamwork within the sales organization.

4. Profit-Sharing Programs

Profit-sharing programs distribute a portion of the company's profits among employees, including sales professionals, based on predefined criteria. This may involve sharing profits generated by specific products, regions, or business units. Profit-sharing aligns the interests of employees with the overall success of the organization, encouraging them to contribute to profitability and long-term growth. However, designing equitable profit-sharing models requires careful consideration of factors such as contribution margins, overhead costs, and revenue allocation.

5. Non-Monetary Incentives

Non-monetary incentives encompass rewards and benefits that do not involve direct financial compensation. Examples include recognition programs, awards ceremonies, career development opportunities, flexible work arrangements, and company-sponsored events. While non-monetary incentives may not directly impact employees' wallets, they can significantly influence morale, job satisfaction, and retention rates. Moreover, non-monetary incentives can complement monetary rewards, providing a well-rounded approach to employee motivation and engagement.

Best Practices for Implementing Incentive Structures

Implementing effective incentive structures requires careful planning, communication, and evaluation. Here are some best practices to consider:

1. Align Incentives with Business Objectives

Ensure that incentive structures are closely aligned with the organization's overarching goals and strategic priorities. Clearly define the desired outcomes and behaviors that will drive success, and design incentives that encourage sales teams to focus their efforts accordingly.

2. Establish Clear and Measurable Targets

Set specific, measurable, achievable, relevant, and time-bound (SMART) targets for sales teams to strive towards. Transparently communicate these targets and regularly track progress against them. Adjust targets as needed to reflect changes in market conditions, business priorities, or performance expectations.

3. Provide Timely and Constructive Feedback

Offer regular feedback and coaching to sales professionals, highlighting areas of strength and opportunities for improvement. Recognize individual and team achievements, and address performance issues promptly and constructively. Feedback should be objective, data-driven, and tailored to individual needs and circumstances.

4. Foster a Culture of Collaboration and Support

Encourage collaboration, knowledge sharing, and mutual support among sales team members. Emphasize the importance of teamwork and collective success, rather than solely focusing on individual performance. Create opportunities for mentorship, peer learning, and cross-functional collaboration to enhance overall sales effectiveness.

5. Evaluate and Adjust Incentive Structures

Continuously monitor the effectiveness of incentive structures through performance metrics, feedback mechanisms, and employee surveys. Solicit input from sales professionals and other stakeholders to identify areas for improvement and refinement. Be prepared to adjust incentive structures as necessary to maintain relevance and effectiveness in a dynamic business environment.

Conclusion

Incentive structures play a critical role in driving sales performance and motivating sales teams to achieve their full potential. By aligning incentives with strategic objectives, setting clear targets, and fostering a supportive culture, organizations can create powerful incentives that inspire excellence, drive results, and fuel sustainable growth. By implementing best practices and continually refining incentive structures based on feedback and evaluation, businesses can optimize sales performance and maximize their competitive advantage in the marketplace.

CHAPTER VI
Leveraging Analytics for Strategic Decision Making

6.1 Utilizing Sales Data for Strategic Planning

6.1.1 Market Segmentation Strategies

Market segmentation is a critical aspect of strategic planning in sales and marketing. It involves dividing a broad target market into smaller, more manageable segments based on distinct characteristics and needs. By understanding the unique preferences and behaviors of each segment, businesses can tailor their sales strategies, products, and messaging to better meet the needs of their customers. In this section, we'll delve into various market segmentation strategies and how businesses can utilize sales data to inform their segmentation efforts effectively.

Understanding Market Segmentation

Market segmentation can be based on various factors, including demographics, psychographics, behavior, geography, and more. By segmenting markets, businesses can identify lucrative opportunities, allocate resources efficiently, and develop targeted marketing campaigns.

Demographic Segmentation:

Demographic segmentation divides markets based on identifiable characteristics such as age, gender, income, occupation, education, and family status. This approach allows businesses to tailor their offerings to specific demographic groups with distinct preferences and purchasing behaviors. For example, a company targeting young professionals may focus on offering trendy, affordable products, while a brand catering to affluent retirees may emphasize luxury and comfort.

Psychographic Segmentation:

Psychographic segmentation categorizes consumers based on their lifestyles, values, beliefs, interests, and personality traits. This approach goes beyond demographic factors to understand the psychological aspects influencing consumer behavior. By identifying psychographic segments, businesses can create marketing messages that resonate with consumers on a deeper level. For instance, a fitness brand might target health-conscious individuals who value sustainability and environmental stewardship, tailoring its messaging to emphasize eco-friendly practices and wellness benefits.

Behavioral Segmentation:

Behavioral segmentation divides consumers based on their purchasing behavior, usage patterns, brand loyalty, and decision-making processes. By analyzing sales data, businesses can identify distinct segments with varying buying habits and preferences. For example, a retailer might segment its customers into frequent shoppers, occasional buyers, and first-time purchasers, then tailor promotions and incentives to encourage repeat purchases and brand loyalty.

Geographic Segmentation:

Geographic segmentation divides markets based on geographic boundaries such as region, city size, climate, or population density. This approach recognizes that consumer needs and preferences can vary significantly based on location. By understanding regional differences, businesses can customize their products, distribution channels, and marketing strategies to better serve each market. For instance, a clothing retailer might offer winter apparel in colder regions and lightweight clothing in warmer climates, reflecting seasonal variations in demand.

Utilizing Sales Data for Segmentation

Sales data serves as a valuable resource for identifying and refining market segments. By analyzing sales transactions, customer interactions, and demographic information, businesses can gain insights into consumer preferences, purchase patterns, and segment-specific behaviors. Here are some key ways to leverage sales data for effective market segmentation:

1. Customer Profiling:

Analyzing sales data allows businesses to create detailed profiles of their customers within each segment. By identifying common traits, preferences, and behaviors, businesses can better understand the needs and motivations driving purchasing decisions. Customer profiles may include demographic information, purchase history, buying frequency, preferred products or services, and communication preferences. This information enables businesses to tailor their marketing efforts and product offerings to align with each segment's unique characteristics.

2. Segmentation Analysis:

Sales data can be analyzed to identify patterns and trends within different market segments. By segmenting sales data based on demographic, psychographic, or behavioral criteria, businesses can assess the performance of each segment and prioritize resources accordingly. For example, businesses may identify segments with high growth potential, low competition, or strong brand affinity, allowing them to allocate marketing budgets and sales efforts more effectively. Segmentation analysis also helps businesses identify underserved or niche markets that may present untapped opportunities for growth.

3. Targeted Marketing Campaigns:

Armed with insights from sales data, businesses can develop targeted marketing campaigns tailored to each market segment. By crafting personalized messages and promotions, businesses can resonate more effectively with their target audience and drive engagement and conversion rates. For example, a retailer targeting young urban professionals may use social media channels and influencer partnerships to promote its products, while a luxury brand targeting affluent consumers may opt for exclusive events and personalized concierge services. Targeted marketing campaigns not only increase the likelihood of conversion but also strengthen brand loyalty and customer relationships.

4. Product Customization and Innovation:

Sales data can provide valuable feedback on product performance and customer preferences within each market segment. By analyzing sales trends, product feedback, and customer reviews, businesses can identify opportunities for product customization and innovation. For example, businesses may introduce new product features, sizes, or variations to better meet the needs of specific segments. Product customization not only enhances customer satisfaction but also drives repeat purchases and strengthens competitive advantage. Additionally, businesses can use sales data to anticipate emerging trends and consumer preferences, enabling them to stay ahead of the competition and capitalize on market opportunities.

Conclusion:

Market segmentation is a fundamental aspect of strategic planning in sales and marketing. By dividing broad target markets into smaller, more manageable segments, businesses can better understand and serve the diverse needs and preferences of their customers.

CHAPTER VI: LEVERAGING ANALYTICS FOR STRATEGIC DECISION MAKING

Leveraging sales data allows businesses to identify and refine market segments effectively, enabling targeted marketing campaigns, product customization, and innovation. By adopting a data-driven approach to market segmentation, businesses can optimize resource allocation, drive customer engagement, and achieve sustainable growth in today's competitive marketplace.

This concludes our discussion on market segmentation strategies and the utilization of sales data for strategic planning. In the next section, we will explore product and pricing strategies to further enhance sales performance and drive business growth.

6.1.2 Product and Pricing Strategies

Welcome6.1.2 Product and Pricing Strategies

Strategic planning in sales hinges significantly on product and pricing strategies. Understanding how to leverage sales data effectively within these realms is paramount for sustainable growth and competitiveness in today's dynamic markets. In this section, we delve into the intricacies of utilizing sales data to inform product development and pricing decisions.

Leveraging Sales Data for Product Development:

1. Identifying High-Performing Products:

   Sales data provides invaluable insights into product performance. By analyzing sales figures, businesses can identify their best-selling products, understand customer preferences, and pinpoint emerging trends. This information is crucial for prioritizing resources and efforts towards developing or enhancing products with proven market demand.

2. Market Gap Analysis:

Sales data enables businesses to conduct comprehensive market gap analyses. By scrutinizing sales trends and customer feedback, organizations can identify areas where demand exceeds supply or where existing products fail to meet consumer expectations. This analysis informs product development strategies, guiding the creation of offerings tailored to fill these gaps and capture untapped market opportunities.

3. Predictive Modeling for Product Innovation:

Advanced analytics techniques, such as predictive modeling, empower businesses to anticipate future market trends and consumer behavior. By extrapolating from historical sales data and incorporating external factors such as demographic shifts or technological advancements, organizations can make informed predictions about which product innovations are likely to resonate with customers. This foresight enables proactive product development strategies that stay ahead of the curve.

Optimizing Pricing Strategies with Sales Data:

1. Dynamic Pricing Adjustments:

Sales data provides real-time insights into market dynamics, allowing businesses to implement dynamic pricing strategies. By monitoring factors such as demand fluctuations, competitor pricing, and customer buying patterns, organizations can adjust prices dynamically to maximize revenue and maintain competitiveness. Dynamic pricing algorithms, fueled by sales data analytics, enable agile pricing decisions that optimize profitability while remaining responsive to market conditions.

2. Value-Based Pricing:

Sales data offers invaluable intelligence on customer perceptions of value and price sensitivity. By correlating sales performance with pricing tiers, businesses can gauge the perceived value of their offerings relative to competitors and identify opportunities for value-based pricing strategies. Analyzing sales data by customer segments or geographic regions allows for nuanced pricing approaches that align with varying preferences and purchasing power, maximizing revenue while maintaining customer satisfaction.

3. Promotion and Discount Optimization:

Sales data illuminates the effectiveness of promotional campaigns and discount strategies. By analyzing the impact of promotions on sales volume and profitability, organizations can refine their promotional tactics to achieve optimal results. A data-driven approach enables businesses to target promotions more effectively, tailoring discounts and incentives to specific customer segments or product categories based on their historical purchasing behavior. This targeted approach minimizes revenue cannibalization while maximizing the ROI of promotional efforts.

Conclusion:

In conclusion, leveraging sales data for strategic product and pricing decisions is imperative for modern businesses seeking to thrive in competitive markets. By harnessing the power of analytics to inform product development and pricing strategies, organizations can align their offerings more closely with customer needs, enhance profitability, and maintain a competitive edge. From identifying market opportunities to optimizing pricing tactics, sales data serves as a invaluable asset for driving strategic growth and innovation. Embracing a data-driven approach empowers businesses to navigate market complexities with confidence and agility, positioning them for long-term success in an ever-evolving business landscape.

6.1.3 Expansion and Diversification Opportunities

Expansion and diversification are critical strategies for businesses aiming to grow sustainably and capture new markets. Utilizing sales data for strategic planning in these areas involves a comprehensive analysis of market trends, customer behavior, and competitive landscapes. By leveraging analytics, businesses can identify lucrative opportunities for expansion into new territories, markets, or product lines, while also minimizing risks associated with such endeavors. This section explores how businesses can harness sales data to identify and capitalize on expansion and diversification opportunities effectively.

Understanding Market Dynamics

Before embarking on any expansion or diversification initiative, businesses must thoroughly understand the dynamics of the markets they intend to enter. Sales data provides invaluable insights into market size, growth rates, customer preferences, and purchasing behavior. By analyzing sales data from existing markets and comparing it with potential target markets, businesses can identify regions or demographics with high growth potential or underserved needs.

Market Segmentation Analysis

Segmentation analysis plays a crucial role in identifying expansion opportunities. By categorizing customers based on various attributes such as demographics, geographic location, or buying behavior, businesses can uncover niche markets or segments that are ripe for exploration. Sales data can reveal patterns and trends within different segments, allowing businesses to tailor their expansion strategies to meet the unique needs of specific customer groups effectively.

Identifying Untapped Potential

Sales data analysis can uncover untapped potential within existing markets or product lines. By examining sales performance metrics such as customer acquisition rates, repeat purchase behavior, and sales growth trajectories, businesses can identify areas where additional investment or focus could yield significant returns. This could involve expanding distribution channels, launching targeted marketing campaigns, or introducing new product variations to capitalize on emerging trends or customer demands.

Competitive Analysis

Understanding the competitive landscape is essential for successful expansion and diversification. Sales data can provide insights into competitors' market share, pricing strategies, and product offerings. Analyzing sales data alongside competitive intelligence allows businesses to identify gaps or weaknesses in competitors' offerings that they can exploit. Additionally, businesses can benchmark their own performance against industry peers to identify areas for improvement and differentiation.

Risk Mitigation Strategies

Expanding into new markets or diversifying product offerings inherently involves risks. Sales data can help businesses assess and mitigate these risks by providing predictive analytics and scenario planning capabilities. By simulating various market scenarios and assessing their potential impact on sales performance, businesses can make more informed decisions and develop contingency plans to mitigate potential risks. Furthermore, continuous monitoring of key performance indicators (KPIs) allows businesses to course-correct quickly if performance deviates from expectations.

Incorporating Customer Feedback

Customer feedback is a valuable source of insights for identifying expansion and diversification opportunities. By integrating customer feedback mechanisms into sales processes, businesses can capture valuable insights into customer preferences, unmet needs, and pain points. Analyzing customer feedback alongside sales data allows businesses to identify opportunities for innovation and differentiation that align with customer expectations.

Employee Engagement

Engaging employees in the strategic planning process is essential for successful expansion and diversification initiatives. Sales teams, in particular, possess firsthand knowledge of market dynamics, customer interactions, and competitor activities. By involving sales teams in the analysis and decision-making process, businesses can leverage their expertise to identify opportunities and challenges more effectively. Additionally, fostering a culture of continuous learning and improvement enables employees to adapt to changing market conditions and contribute innovative ideas for growth.

Conclusion

Utilizing sales data for strategic planning is essential for identifying and capitalizing on expansion and diversification opportunities. By leveraging analytics to understand market dynamics, segment customers, analyze competitors, and mitigate risks, businesses can develop more informed and effective growth strategies. Incorporating customer feedback and engaging employees in the strategic planning process enhances decision-making and ensures alignment with market realities. Ultimately, businesses that harness the power of sales data to drive strategic expansion and diversification are better positioned to achieve sustainable growth and competitive advantage in today's dynamic business environment.

6.2 Adapting to Market Changes

6.2.1 Agility in Decision Making

In today's dynamic business environment, the ability to swiftly adapt to market changes is crucial for sustained success. Agile decision-making empowers organizations to respond promptly to evolving market conditions, customer preferences, and competitive landscapes. This section delves into the significance of agility in decision-making processes and explores strategies to foster agility within an organization.

Importance of Agility in Decision Making

Agility in decision making refers to the capacity to make quick, informed decisions in response to changing circumstances. In a rapidly evolving market, where disruptions and innovations are constant, agile decision making enables businesses to seize opportunities and mitigate risks efficiently. Here are some key reasons why agility is essential:

1. Competitive Advantage:

Agile organizations can capitalize on emerging trends and swiftly adjust their strategies to stay ahead of competitors. By making timely decisions, they can preempt market shifts and exploit new opportunities, thereby gaining a competitive edge.

2. Enhanced Responsiveness:

Market dynamics can change rapidly due to factors such as technological advancements, regulatory changes, or shifts in consumer behavior. Agile decision making ensures that organizations can respond promptly to these changes, minimizing disruption to their operations and maintaining customer satisfaction.

3. Innovation Enablement:

Agility fosters a culture of experimentation and innovation within an organization. By encouraging flexibility and adaptability, businesses can explore new ideas and approaches, leading to the development of innovative products, services, and processes.

4. Risk Mitigation:

In volatile markets, unforeseen risks can arise suddenly, posing threats to business continuity. Agile decision making allows organizations to identify and address risks proactively, thereby reducing their potential impact and enhancing resilience.

Strategies for Enhancing Agility

Achieving agility in decision making requires a combination of organizational culture, processes, and technologies. Here are some strategies to foster agility within your organization:

1. Empower Cross-Functional Teams:

Encourage collaboration among diverse teams representing various departments and functions within the organization. Cross-functional teams bring together different perspectives and expertise, enabling faster decision making and effective problem-solving.

2. Decentralize Decision Making:

Empower employees at all levels to make decisions within their areas of responsibility. Decentralization distributes decision-making authority across the organization, enabling quicker responses to market changes and fostering a sense of ownership among employees.

3. Implement Agile Methodologies:

Adopt agile methodologies such as Scrum or Kanban to streamline decision-making processes and project management. These methodologies emphasize iterative development, frequent feedback loops, and adaptive planning, enabling teams to respond rapidly to evolving requirements and priorities.

4. Invest in Data Analytics:

Utilize data analytics tools and techniques to gather insights into market trends, customer behavior, and competitive intelligence. Data-driven decision making enables organizations to make informed choices based on real-time information, enhancing agility and reducing reliance on intuition or guesswork.

5. Foster a Culture of Learning:

Encourage continuous learning and skill development among employees to adapt to changing market dynamics. Provide opportunities for training, knowledge sharing, and experimentation, fostering a culture of curiosity, innovation, and adaptability.

6. Embrace Digital Transformation:

Leverage digital technologies to automate processes, streamline workflows, and enable remote collaboration. Digital transformation enhances organizational agility by enabling faster communication, decision making, and resource allocation, irrespective of geographical constraints.

Case Study: Agile Decision Making in Action

To illustrate the benefits of agile decision making, let's consider the case of Company X, a multinational retail corporation facing intense competition in the e-commerce sector. Recognizing the need to adapt to changing consumer preferences and technological advancements, Company X implemented agile principles across its operations.

Situation:

Company X observed a shift in consumer behavior towards online shopping, driven by convenience and accessibility. To remain competitive in the rapidly evolving e-commerce landscape, the company needed to enhance its digital capabilities and expand its online presence.

Approach:

1. Cross-Functional Collaboration: Company X formed cross-functional teams comprising members from marketing, IT, operations, and customer service departments to drive its e-commerce initiatives. These teams collaborated closely to identify market trends, develop digital strategies, and implement innovative solutions.

2. Decentralized Decision Making: Empowered by senior leadership, frontline employees were given the autonomy to make decisions regarding customer engagement, product offerings, and marketing campaigns. This decentralized approach enabled rapid responses to customer feedback and market dynamics, resulting in increased agility and customer satisfaction.

3. Agile Methodologies: Company X adopted agile methodologies such as Scrum to manage its e-commerce projects effectively. By breaking down large initiatives into smaller, manageable tasks and conducting regular sprints, the teams were able to iterate quickly, adapt to changing requirements, and deliver value to customers at a faster pace.

4. Data-Driven Insights: Leveraging advanced analytics tools, Company X analyzed customer data, website metrics, and market trends to gain actionable insights. These insights guided decision making, enabling the company to personalize its offerings, optimize its digital channels, and anticipate future trends in the e-commerce space.

Results:

By embracing agile decision making, Company X achieved significant improvements in its e-commerce performance:

- Increased Online Sales: The company experienced a significant uptick in online sales, driven by enhanced digital experiences, targeted marketing campaigns, and personalized recommendations.

- Improved Customer Satisfaction: By responding promptly to customer feedback and preferences, Company X improved its overall customer satisfaction ratings and loyalty, leading to higher retention rates and repeat purchases.

- Accelerated Time-to-Market: Agile methodologies enabled faster development and deployment of new features and functionalities, allowing Company X to stay ahead of competitors and capitalize on emerging opportunities in the e-commerce market.

Conclusion

Agility in decision making is imperative for navigating the complexities of today's business landscape. By fostering a culture of collaboration, experimentation, and data-driven insights, organizations can enhance their adaptability, resilience, and competitive advantage. Embracing agile principles empowers businesses to thrive in an ever-changing environment, driving innovation, growth, and customer success.

6.2.2 Scenario Planning

Scenario planning is a vital tool for businesses to navigate uncertainties and prepare for various potential futures. In a rapidly changing market landscape, where disruptions are common, scenario planning offers a structured approach to anticipate and respond to different outcomes. By envisioning multiple scenarios, businesses can better understand potential challenges and opportunities, enabling them to make informed decisions and develop robust strategies. This section explores the importance of scenario planning and outlines key steps for its implementation.

Understanding Scenario Planning

Scenario planning involves the creation of plausible, alternative futures based on different combinations of critical uncertainties. Unlike traditional forecasting methods that rely on historical data and linear projections, scenario planning acknowledges the complexity and uncertainty inherent in the business environment. It encourages stakeholders to think creatively and consider a range of possibilities, including disruptive events and paradigm shifts.

Benefits of Scenario Planning

1. Enhanced Strategic Agility: Scenario planning allows organizations to adapt quickly to changing circumstances by considering various plausible scenarios in advance. By identifying potential risks and opportunities, businesses can adjust their strategies proactively, minimizing the impact of unforeseen events.

2. Improved Decision Making: By exploring different scenarios, decision-makers gain a deeper understanding of the factors influencing their business environment. This insight enables more informed decision-making, as leaders can evaluate the potential consequences of their choices across multiple scenarios.

3. Risk Mitigation: Scenario planning helps businesses identify and prepare for potential risks, reducing their vulnerability to unexpected events. By developing contingency plans and building resilience, organizations can mitigate the impact of adverse scenarios and maintain business continuity.

4. Strategic Innovation: Through scenario planning, organizations can uncover new opportunities and innovative solutions that may not have been apparent in a single forecast. By challenging conventional thinking and exploring alternative futures, businesses can drive strategic innovation and gain a competitive edge.

5. Enhanced Stakeholder Alignment: Scenario planning facilitates discussions among stakeholders, fostering alignment and consensus on strategic priorities. By engaging diverse perspectives and exploring different scenarios collaboratively, organizations can build a shared understanding of the future landscape and align their actions accordingly.

Key Steps in Scenario Planning

1. Identify Critical Uncertainties: Begin by identifying the key uncertainties that could significantly impact your business. These uncertainties may include technological advancements, regulatory changes, market trends, geopolitical events, or socio-economic shifts.

2. Develop Scenarios: Based on the identified uncertainties, create a set of plausible scenarios representing different combinations of potential outcomes. Each scenario should describe a coherent narrative of how the future might unfold, considering both quantitative and qualitative factors.

3. Assess Implications: Evaluate the potential implications of each scenario on your business, including opportunities, risks, challenges, and strategic priorities. Consider how each scenario would affect your customers, competitors, suppliers, and other stakeholders.

4. Develop Strategies: Develop strategies and action plans to respond effectively to each scenario. Identify specific initiatives, resource allocations, and decision criteria tailored to the unique challenges and opportunities presented by each scenario.

5. Monitor and Adapt: Continuously monitor the external environment for signals and indicators that may signal shifts in the likelihood or impact of different scenarios. Regularly review and update your scenarios and strategies to reflect evolving market conditions and new insights.

Case Study: Scenario Planning in Action

To illustrate the practical application of scenario planning, let's consider a fictional case study of a global automotive manufacturer facing uncertainty in the transition to electric vehicles (EVs).

Background:

XYZ Motors is a leading automotive manufacturer known for its gasoline-powered vehicles. With growing concerns about climate change and increasing government regulations on emissions, the company is facing pressure to transition to electric vehicles (EVs). However, the market for EVs is still evolving, with uncertainties surrounding technological advancements, consumer preferences, infrastructure development, and regulatory policies.

Scenario Development:

XYZ Motors identifies four critical uncertainties influencing the transition to EVs:

1. Technological Advancements: Will there be breakthroughs in battery technology, charging infrastructure, and vehicle performance?

2. Consumer Adoption: How quickly will consumers adopt EVs, and what factors will drive their purchasing decisions?

3. Regulatory Environment: What policies and regulations will governments implement to promote EV adoption and reduce carbon emissions?

4. Competitive Landscape: How will existing automotive manufacturers and new entrants compete in the EV market, and what strategies will they pursue?

Based on these uncertainties, XYZ Motors develops four scenarios:

1. Technological Revolution: Breakthroughs in battery technology lead to affordable, long-range EVs with fast-charging capabilities. Consumer demand surges, supported by government incentives and infrastructure investments. XYZ Motors rapidly transitions its production to EVs and gains a competitive advantage in the market.

2. Consumer Skepticism: Despite technological advancements, consumer adoption of EVs remains slow due to concerns about range anxiety, charging infrastructure, and vehicle affordability. XYZ Motors cautiously invests in EV production while maintaining its focus on traditional vehicles.

3. Regulatory Mandates: Stringent emissions regulations and government mandates accelerate the transition to EVs, forcing automakers to prioritize electric vehicle development. XYZ Motors ramps up its EV production to comply with regulations but faces challenges in meeting consumer demand and infrastructure requirements.

4. Competitive Disruption: New entrants disrupt the automotive market with innovative EV offerings, challenging established players like XYZ Motors. Traditional manufacturers struggle to adapt to the changing landscape, leading to consolidation and strategic partnerships. XYZ Motors diversifies its product portfolio and explores collaborations to remain competitive.

Strategy Development:

For each scenario, XYZ Motors develops tailored strategies to address the opportunities and challenges presented:

1. Technological Revolution: Invest heavily in EV research and development, expand charging infrastructure, and launch aggressive marketing campaigns to capitalize on growing consumer demand for EVs.

2. Consumer Skepticism: Continue investing in gasoline-powered vehicles while gradually introducing EV models to test consumer preferences. Focus on improving EV affordability, range, and charging infrastructure to address consumer concerns.

3. Regulatory Mandates: Accelerate EV production and invest in sustainable manufacturing processes to comply with emissions regulations. Collaborate with governments and industry partners to advocate for supportive policies and infrastructure investments.

4. Competitive Disruption: Strengthen partnerships with technology firms and start-ups to access innovative EV technologies. Diversify product offerings to appeal to different market segments and explore strategic alliances to enhance competitiveness.

Implementation and Monitoring:

XYZ Motors implements its strategies across different scenarios while closely monitoring market developments and adjusting its approach as needed. By regularly reviewing its scenarios and strategies, XYZ Motors remains agile and resilient in the face of uncertainty, positioning itself for long-term success in the evolving automotive landscape.

Conclusion

Scenario planning is a powerful tool for businesses to navigate uncertainty, anticipate challenges, and capitalize on opportunities in a rapidly changing market environment. By envisioning alternative futures, developing robust strategies, and fostering organizational agility, businesses can enhance their resilience and drive sustainable growth. Embracing scenario planning as a core strategic practice enables organizations to thrive amidst uncertainty, adapt to market changes, and achieve their long-term objectives.

6.2.3 Risk Management Strategies

Risk management is a critical aspect of adapting to market changes. In a dynamic business environment, uncertainties are inevitable, ranging from changes in consumer behavior to unexpected regulatory shifts or economic downturns. Effective risk management strategies help businesses anticipate, assess, and mitigate these risks to safeguard their performance and viability. This section explores various risk management strategies that sales teams can employ to navigate through market uncertainties.

1. Identifying Risks:

Before devising risk management strategies, it is essential to identify potential risks that could impact sales performance. Risks can stem from various sources, including market volatility, technological disruptions, competitive pressures, regulatory changes, and supply chain disruptions. Sales teams should conduct comprehensive risk assessments to understand the nature and potential impact of these risks on their operations.

2. Risk Assessment and Prioritization:

Not all risks carry the same level of impact or likelihood. Therefore, sales organizations need to prioritize risks based on their potential severity and likelihood of occurrence. This involves quantifying risks through techniques such as probability analysis, impact assessment, and risk mapping. By prioritizing risks, sales teams can allocate resources more effectively and focus their attention on mitigating high-priority risks first.

3. Diversification Strategies:

Diversification is a fundamental risk management strategy that involves spreading sales activities across multiple markets, products, or customer segments. By diversifying their sales portfolio, organizations can reduce their exposure to risks associated with a single market or product line. For instance, expanding into new geographic regions or targeting different customer demographics can help mitigate the impact of regional economic downturns or shifts in consumer preferences.

4. Hedging Against Market Fluctuations:

Sales teams can mitigate risks arising from market fluctuations by employing hedging strategies. For example, businesses can enter into forward contracts or options to lock in favorable exchange rates, commodity prices, or interest rates. By hedging against adverse market movements, organizations can protect their profit margins and minimize the impact of external uncertainties on their financial performance.

5. Contingency Planning:

Contingency planning involves developing alternative courses of action to address potential risks and mitigate their impact on sales operations. This may include creating backup supply chain routes, establishing alternative distribution channels, or securing alternative sources of funding. By proactively planning for contingencies, sales teams can respond swiftly to unforeseen events and maintain business continuity even in challenging circumstances.

6. Monitoring and Early Warning Systems:

Implementing robust monitoring systems and early warning indicators is essential for detecting emerging risks promptly. Sales organizations can leverage data analytics and predictive modeling techniques to identify early signs of market disruptions or shifts in customer behavior. By monitoring key performance metrics and market trends in real-time, businesses can proactively adjust their strategies to mitigate potential risks before they escalate into significant threats.

7. Collaboration and Information Sharing:

Effective risk management requires collaboration and information sharing across different functional areas within the organization. Sales teams should work closely with other departments, such as finance, operations, and marketing, to align risk management efforts and leverage collective expertise. Cross-functional collaboration enables organizations to identify risks more comprehensively and develop holistic risk mitigation strategies that address multiple dimensions of risk.

8. Scenario Planning and Stress Testing:

Scenario planning involves simulating various hypothetical scenarios to assess their potential impact on sales performance. By exploring alternative future scenarios, sales teams can identify vulnerabilities and devise contingency plans to mitigate risks associated with each scenario. Additionally, stress testing involves subjecting sales strategies and business models to extreme scenarios to evaluate their resilience and identify potential weaknesses. Through scenario planning and stress testing, organizations can enhance their preparedness for a wide range of market conditions and uncertainties.

9. Continuous Evaluation and Adaptation:

Risk management is not a one-time exercise but rather an ongoing process that requires continuous evaluation and adaptation. Sales teams should regularly review and update their risk management strategies in response to changing market dynamics, emerging risks, and lessons learned from past experiences. By fostering a culture of continuous improvement and agility, organizations can enhance their ability to anticipate and mitigate risks effectively.

Conclusion:

In conclusion, adapting to market changes requires robust risk management strategies that enable sales organizations to anticipate, assess, and mitigate various uncertainties. By identifying risks, prioritizing them, and implementing proactive risk mitigation measures, businesses can enhance their resilience and agility in the face of market volatility and disruptions. Through diversification, hedging, contingency planning, and collaborative efforts, sales teams can navigate through uncertainties and sustain long-term growth and profitability in an ever-changing business environment. Continuous evaluation, adaptation, and learning are essential for ensuring that risk management strategies remain effective and aligned with evolving market dynamics. By integrating risk management into their strategic decision-making processes, sales organizations can effectively manage uncertainties and capitalize on opportunities for growth and competitive advantage.

6.3 Incorporating Feedback Loops

6.3.1 Continuous Improvement Processes

Continuous improvement is the backbone of any successful organization. It involves constantly refining processes, products, and services to enhance efficiency, quality, and customer satisfaction. In the context of sales metrics and analytics, incorporating continuous improvement processes is paramount to staying competitive in a rapidly evolving market landscape. This section delves into the principles of continuous improvement and how they can be effectively integrated into sales strategies through the lens of data-driven decision-making.

Understanding Continuous Improvement

Continuous improvement, often associated with methodologies such as Lean Six Sigma, Kaizen, or Total Quality Management (TQM), emphasizes the ongoing effort to enhance processes incrementally. At its core, continuous improvement revolves around the PDCA (Plan-Do-Check-Act) cycle, a systematic approach for problem-solving and process optimization.

1. Plan:

   - **Define Objectives:** Clearly outline the goals of the improvement initiative. Whether it's reducing sales cycle times, improving lead conversion rates, or enhancing customer satisfaction, setting specific, measurable, achievable, relevant, and time-bound (SMART) objectives is crucial.

   - **Identify Metrics:** Determine the key performance indicators (KPIs) that will gauge the success of the improvement efforts. These metrics may include sales revenue, customer acquisition cost (CAC), customer lifetime value (CLV), and sales conversion rates.

- **Allocate Resources:** Allocate the necessary resources, including personnel, technology, and budget, to support the improvement initiatives effectively.

2. Do:

- **Implement Changes:** Execute the planned improvements, whether they involve process reengineering, technology integration, or skill development among sales teams.

- **Train and Educate:** Provide training and education to employees to equip them with the skills and knowledge required to adapt to the changes effectively.

- **Test on a Small Scale:** Conduct pilot tests or trials on a small scale to assess the effectiveness of the proposed changes before full-scale implementation.

3. Check:

- **Monitor Progress:** Continuously monitor the performance metrics to evaluate the impact of the implemented changes. This may involve real-time tracking through analytics dashboards or periodic reviews.

- **Gather Feedback:** Solicit feedback from stakeholders, including sales teams, customers, and partners, to gain insights into the effectiveness of the improvements and identify areas for further refinement.

- **Identify Issues:** Identify any deviations from the expected outcomes or any unforeseen challenges that may have arisen during the implementation phase.

4. Act:

- **Adjust and Iterate:** Based on the findings from the monitoring and feedback processes, make necessary adjustments to the improvement initiatives. This may involve refining processes, reallocating resources, or revising objectives.

- **Scale Up:** Once the effectiveness of the improvements has been validated, scale up the changes across the organization to realize broader benefits.

- **Celebrate Success:** Recognize and celebrate the achievements and milestones reached through the continuous improvement efforts. This helps foster a culture of innovation and excellence within the organization.

Integrating Data Analytics into Continuous Improvement

Data analytics plays a pivotal role in facilitating continuous improvement processes within sales organizations. By leveraging data-driven insights, organizations can identify areas for improvement, measure the impact of changes, and make informed decisions to drive performance enhancements. Below are some key strategies for integrating data analytics into continuous improvement initiatives:

1. Data Collection and Analysis:

- **Capture Relevant Metrics:** Collect and analyze a diverse range of sales metrics, including conversion rates, customer churn rates, sales pipeline velocity, and sales cycle lengths. Ensure that the data collected aligns with the objectives of the improvement initiatives.

- **Utilize Advanced Analytics:** Employ advanced analytics techniques, such as predictive modeling, machine learning, and data mining, to uncover patterns, trends, and correlations within the sales data. These insights can provide valuable guidance for identifying improvement opportunities and predicting future sales performance.

2. Root Cause Analysis:

- **Identify Underlying Factors:** Conduct root cause analysis to uncover the underlying factors contributing to performance gaps or inefficiencies within the sales processes. This may involve analyzing historical data, conducting surveys or interviews, and using techniques such as fishbone diagrams or 5 Whys analysis.

- **Prioritize Improvement Opportunities:** Prioritize improvement opportunities based on their potential impact on key business objectives and their feasibility for implementation. Focus on addressing root causes rather than merely treating symptoms to achieve sustainable improvements.

3. Continuous Monitoring and Feedback:

- **Real-time Monitoring:** Implement real-time monitoring systems that provide up-to-date insights into sales performance metrics. This allows organizations to identify issues promptly and take corrective actions as needed.

- **Feedback Mechanisms:** Establish feedback mechanisms, such as customer satisfaction surveys, sales team feedback loops, and performance reviews, to gather insights from stakeholders at various touchpoints. Analyze this feedback to identify areas for improvement and make data-driven decisions.

4. Predictive Analytics for Future Performance:

- **Forecasting and Predictive Modeling:** Leverage predictive analytics techniques to forecast future sales performance and identify potential risks and opportunities. This enables organizations to proactively adjust their strategies and tactics to optimize outcomes.

- **Scenario Planning:** Use scenario planning and sensitivity analysis to simulate various what-if scenarios and assess their potential impact on sales performance. This helps organizations prepare for different eventualities and develop contingency plans accordingly.

Case Study: Implementing Continuous Improvement with Data Analytics

To illustrate the practical application of continuous improvement processes with data analytics, let's consider a hypothetical case study of a software-as-a-service (SaaS) company looking to improve its sales performance.

Objective: The company aims to increase its customer acquisition rate and reduce churn by optimizing its sales processes and enhancing customer engagement.

Plan:

- **Define Objectives:** Increase customer acquisition rate by 15% within the next quarter and reduce customer churn by 10%.

- **Identify Metrics:** Key metrics include customer acquisition cost (CAC), customer lifetime value (CLV), lead-to-customer conversion rate, and customer churn rate.

- **Allocate Resources:** Allocate additional resources for sales training, marketing campaigns, and customer success initiatives.

Do:

- **Implement Changes:** Streamline the lead management process, implement personalized marketing campaigns, and enhance customer support services.

- **Train and Educate:** Provide sales teams with training on consultative selling techniques and product knowledge. Educate customers on best practices for utilizing the software effectively.

- **Test on a Small Scale:** Pilot test the new lead management process and marketing campaigns with a selected segment of customers.

Check:

- **Monitor Progress:** Track key metrics using a sales analytics dashboard to assess the impact of the implemented changes on customer acquisition and retention.

- **Gather Feedback:** Collect feedback from sales teams, customers, and support staff to identify any challenges or areas for improvement.

- **Identify Issues:** Identify bottlenecks in the sales funnel, customer pain points, and factors contributing to churn.

Act:

- **Adjust and Iterate:** Based on feedback and performance metrics, refine the sales processes, adjust marketing strategies, and enhance customer support mechanisms.

- **Scale Up:** Roll out the optimized processes and strategies across all customer segments. Implement feedback loops to continuously monitor and adjust performance.

- **Celebrate Success:** Recognize and reward sales teams for their contributions to achieving the improvement objectives. Share success stories and best practices to inspire a culture of continuous improvement.

Conclusion

Incorporating feedback loops and continuous improvement processes into sales strategies is essential for organizations to adapt to changing market dynamics, enhance performance, and drive sustainable growth. By leveraging data analytics, organizations can gain valuable insights into sales performance, identify improvement opportunities, and make informed decisions to optimize their processes and achieve their business objectives. With a commitment to continuous improvement and a data-driven approach, organizations can stay ahead of the competition and thrive in today's highly competitive marketplace.

6.3.2 Customer Feedback Integration

Customer feedback integration is a vital component of any successful sales strategy. In today's competitive business landscape, understanding customer needs, preferences, and pain points is crucial for driving sales growth and maintaining a loyal customer base. By incorporating feedback loops into your sales analytics framework, you can gain valuable insights into customer satisfaction levels, identify areas for improvement, and make data-driven decisions to enhance the overall customer experience.

The Importance of Customer Feedback

Customer feedback serves as a direct line of communication between businesses and their customers. It provides valuable insights into how customers perceive products, services, and brand interactions. By actively soliciting and analyzing customer feedback, organizations can:

- Identify strengths and weaknesses: Customer feedback helps businesses understand what they are doing well and areas where they need improvement. By identifying strengths, businesses can capitalize on their competitive advantages. Conversely, recognizing weaknesses enables organizations to address issues and enhance their offerings.

- Enhance product/service quality: Customer feedback allows businesses to gather insights into how customers use their products or services. By understanding customer pain points and preferences, organizations can make informed decisions to improve product quality, functionality, and features.

- Drive innovation: Customer feedback often contains suggestions and ideas for product enhancements or new offerings. By listening to customer suggestions, businesses can innovate and develop solutions that meet evolving customer needs and preferences.

- Foster customer loyalty: When customers feel heard and valued, they are more likely to develop a sense of loyalty towards a brand. By actively engaging with customer feedback and addressing concerns promptly, businesses can strengthen customer relationships and foster loyalty over time.

Strategies for Effective Customer Feedback Integration

Integrating customer feedback into your sales analytics framework requires a systematic approach. Here are some strategies to effectively incorporate customer feedback into your sales strategy:

1. Implement multi-channel feedback collection methods:

Utilize a variety of channels, such as surveys, social media, online reviews, and direct communication channels, to collect feedback from customers. By offering multiple avenues for feedback, you can capture a diverse range of customer perspectives and preferences.

2. Leverage technology for automated feedback collection and analysis:

Invest in customer feedback management software or tools that allow for automated feedback collection, analysis, and reporting. These tools can streamline the feedback process, enabling businesses to gather insights in real-time and respond promptly to customer concerns.

3. Actively listen to customer feedback:

Make it a priority to actively listen to customer feedback and demonstrate a willingness to address customer concerns. Act on feedback promptly and transparently communicate the steps taken to address customer issues. By showing customers that their feedback is valued and acted upon, you can build trust and credibility.

4. Segment and analyze feedback data:

Segment customer feedback data based on various factors such as demographics, purchasing behavior, and satisfaction levels. Analyze feedback trends and patterns to identify common themes, emerging issues, and areas for improvement. By segmenting feedback data, businesses can tailor their responses and strategies to specific customer segments.

5. Integrate feedback into decision-making processes:

Incorporate customer feedback into strategic decision-making processes across the organization. Use feedback insights to inform product development, marketing strategies, sales tactics, and customer service initiatives. By integrating customer feedback into decision-making processes, businesses can align their efforts with customer needs and preferences.

6. Continuously monitor and evaluate feedback loops:

Establish a feedback loop monitoring system to track the effectiveness of your feedback integration efforts. Regularly monitor key metrics such as customer satisfaction scores, Net Promoter Score (NPS), and customer retention rates. Evaluate the impact of feedback-driven initiatives on sales performance and overall business outcomes.

Case Study: Incorporating Customer Feedback into Sales Strategy

To illustrate the importance of customer feedback integration, let's consider a hypothetical case study of a software company looking to improve its sales performance through customer-centric strategies.

Company Background:

XYZ Software is a leading provider of cloud-based project management software. Despite having a robust product offering, the company has been experiencing a decline in sales and customer satisfaction levels in recent months.

Challenges:

- Decreasing sales revenue and market share.

- Rising customer complaints regarding product usability and functionality.

- Increased competition from new market entrants offering similar products.

Approach:

To address these challenges, XYZ Software decides to prioritize customer feedback integration into its sales strategy. The company implements the following steps:

1. Multi-channel feedback collection: XYZ Software launches an online survey to gather feedback from existing customers regarding their experiences with the software. Additionally, the company actively monitors social media channels and online review platforms for customer feedback.

2. Feedback analysis: The feedback collected is analyzed using sentiment analysis tools to identify common themes and pain points. Key areas of concern include usability issues, lack of certain features, and slow response times from customer support.

3. Actionable insights: XYZ Software uses the insights gained from feedback analysis to prioritize areas for improvement. The product development team works on enhancing the software's user interface, adding new features requested by customers, and implementing a customer support escalation process to address issues more efficiently.

4. Communication and transparency: The company communicates with customers transparently about the steps taken to address their feedback. Regular updates are provided through email newsletters, social media posts, and in-product notifications.

5. Continuous improvement: XYZ Software establishes a feedback loop monitoring system to track the impact of feedback-driven initiatives on sales performance and customer satisfaction. Key metrics such as NPS scores, customer retention rates, and sales revenue are monitored regularly.

Results:

By incorporating customer feedback into its sales strategy, XYZ Software achieves the following results:

- Improved product usability and functionality, leading to higher customer satisfaction levels.

- Increased customer retention rates and loyalty, resulting in a higher lifetime value per customer.

- Enhanced sales performance and market competitiveness, with a noticeable increase in sales revenue and market share.

Conclusion

Incorporating customer feedback into your sales strategy is essential for driving business growth, enhancing customer satisfaction, and maintaining a competitive edge in the marketplace. By actively listening to customer feedback, analyzing insights, and integrating feedback into decision-making processes, businesses can align their efforts with customer needs and preferences. Ultimately, a customer-centric approach to sales analytics enables organizations to build stronger relationships with customers, drive sales growth, and achieve long-term success in today's dynamic business environment.

6.3.3 Employee Engagement and Feedback Mechanisms

Employee engagement and feedback mechanisms are integral components of a successful sales organization. In today's dynamic business landscape, where competition is fierce and customer demands are constantly evolving, organizations must prioritize the engagement and satisfaction of their sales teams. Engaged employees are more productive, innovative, and committed to achieving organizational goals. Moreover, they play a crucial role in providing valuable insights and feedback that can drive continuous improvement and foster a culture of excellence within the sales organization.

This section explores the importance of employee engagement and feedback mechanisms in the context of sales metrics and analytics. We will delve into strategies for fostering employee engagement, implementing effective feedback mechanisms, and leveraging employee insights to enhance sales performance.

Importance of Employee Engagement in Sales Organizations

Employee engagement refers to the emotional commitment and dedication that employees have towards their work and the organization. Engaged employees are passionate about their roles, aligned with the organization's goals, and willing to go the extra mile to contribute to its success. In a sales context, employee engagement is particularly crucial, as sales teams are at the forefront of driving revenue and building customer relationships.

Research has consistently shown that engaged sales teams outperform their disengaged counterparts in key metrics such as sales revenue, customer satisfaction, and employee retention. Engaged sales representatives are more likely to deliver exceptional customer experiences, leading to higher customer loyalty and repeat business. Furthermore, engaged employees are more resilient in the face of challenges and are better equipped to adapt to changing market dynamics.

Strategies for Fostering Employee Engagement

Fostering employee engagement requires a holistic approach that encompasses various aspects of organizational culture, leadership, and employee development. Here are some strategies for cultivating engagement within the sales organization:

1. Cultivate a Positive Work Environment:

 - Foster a culture of trust, transparency, and respect where employees feel valued and appreciated.

 - Provide opportunities for professional growth and development, including training programs, mentorship, and career advancement paths.

 - Recognize and reward employees for their achievements and contributions to the organization's success.

2. Empowerment and Autonomy:

 - Empower sales representatives to make decisions and take ownership of their work.

 - Provide autonomy in setting goals, managing priorities, and executing sales strategies.

 - Encourage innovation and creativity by soliciting input from employees and implementing their ideas.

3. Open Communication Channels:

- Establish open and transparent communication channels for sharing information, updates, and feedback.

- Encourage regular one-on-one meetings between managers and employees to discuss goals, challenges, and career aspirations.

- Foster a culture of constructive feedback where employees feel comfortable providing input and raising concerns.

4. Promote Work-Life Balance:

- Recognize the importance of work-life balance and support employees in managing their personal and professional commitments.

- Offer flexible work arrangements, such as remote work options or flexible hours, to accommodate diverse needs and preferences.

- Provide resources and support for employee well-being, including access to mental health resources, wellness programs, and stress management initiatives.

5. Lead by Example:

- Leadership plays a critical role in shaping organizational culture and employee engagement.

- Lead by example and demonstrate behaviors that align with the organization's values and priorities.

- Provide leadership training and development opportunities to empower managers to effectively engage and motivate their teams.

Implementing Effective Feedback Mechanisms

Feedback is essential for driving improvement and performance excellence within the sales organization. Effective feedback mechanisms enable employees to receive timely, constructive feedback on their performance, identify areas for growth and development, and track progress towards their goals. Additionally, feedback channels provide a valuable opportunity for employees to share their insights, suggestions, and concerns with organizational leadership.

1. Performance Reviews and Coaching:

- Conduct regular performance reviews to assess sales representatives' performance against key metrics and objectives.

- Provide specific, actionable feedback to help employees understand their strengths and areas for improvement.

- Offer ongoing coaching and development opportunities to support employees in achieving their goals and enhancing their skills.

2. 360-Degree Feedback:

- Implement a 360-degree feedback process where employees receive feedback from multiple sources, including peers, managers, and customers.

- This comprehensive feedback approach provides a holistic view of an employee's performance and behavior, fostering self-awareness and growth.

3. Pulse Surveys and Feedback Platforms:

- Use pulse surveys and feedback platforms to gather regular input from employees on various aspects of their work experience, including job satisfaction, engagement, and organizational culture.

- These short, anonymous surveys provide valuable insights into employees' perceptions and enable organizations to identify areas for improvement.

4. Town Hall Meetings and Open Forums:

- Host regular town hall meetings and open forums where employees can voice their opinions, ask questions, and share feedback with organizational leadership.

- Create a safe and inclusive environment where all employees feel comfortable expressing their views and contributing to meaningful discussions.

5. Continuous Improvement Processes:

- Establish a culture of continuous improvement where feedback is used to drive positive change and innovation within the organization.

- Encourage employees to participate in problem-solving initiatives and suggest ideas for process improvement and efficiency gains.

Leveraging Employee Insights for Sales Performance

Employee insights are a valuable source of information that can provide valuable perspectives on customer needs, market trends, and competitive dynamics. By tapping into the collective knowledge and expertise of their sales teams, organizations can gain a deeper understanding of their target market and make more informed decisions to drive sales performance.

1. Sales Team Collaboration:

- Foster collaboration and knowledge-sharing among sales team members to leverage their collective insights and experiences.

- Encourage cross-functional collaboration with other departments, such as marketing, product development, and customer service, to align sales strategies with broader organizational goals.

2. Sales Meetings and Brainstorming Sessions:

- Hold regular sales meetings and brainstorming sessions where employees can discuss challenges, share best practices, and brainstorm innovative solutions.

- Encourage active participation and idea generation to tap into the creativity and expertise of the sales team.

3. Customer Feedback Integration:

- Encourage sales representatives to actively seek feedback from customers and incorporate it into their sales strategies.

- Use customer feedback to identify emerging trends, anticipate customer needs, and tailor sales approaches to meet customer preferences.

4. Competitive Intelligence Gathering:

- Equip sales teams with the tools and resources they need to gather competitive intelligence and stay informed about market trends and competitor activities.

- Encourage sales representatives to share insights and observations about competitor strategies, product offerings, and pricing to inform strategic decision-making.

5. Data-Driven Insights:

- Leverage sales data and analytics to generate actionable insights that inform sales strategies and tactics.

- Provide sales teams with access to dashboards, reports, and analytics tools that enable them to track performance metrics, identify opportunities, and make data-driven decisions.

Conclusion

Employee engagement and feedback mechanisms are essential drivers of success in the modern sales organization. By prioritizing employee engagement, fostering a culture of open communication, and implementing effective feedback mechanisms, organizations can empower their sales teams to achieve higher levels of performance, innovation, and customer satisfaction. Moreover, by leveraging employee insights and expertise, organizations can gain a competitive edge in today's fast-paced and dynamic business environment. By investing in the engagement and development of their sales teams, organizations can position themselves for long-term success and sustainable growth.

Appendices

Useful Software and Platforms

In today's digital age, sales organizations have access to a wide range of software and platforms designed to streamline processes, enhance productivity, and improve decision-making. From customer relationship management (CRM) systems to sales analytics tools, the following list highlights some of the most useful software and platforms for sales teams:

Customer Relationship Management (CRM) Systems:

1. Salesforce: One of the most popular CRM platforms, Salesforce offers a comprehensive suite of sales, marketing, and customer service tools. It enables sales teams to manage customer relationships, track leads and opportunities, and collaborate effectively across the organization.

2. HubSpot CRM: HubSpot CRM provides a user-friendly interface and powerful features for managing contacts, deals, and tasks. It integrates seamlessly with other HubSpot tools, such as marketing automation and customer service, to create a unified platform for sales and marketing teams.

3. Microsoft Dynamics 365: Microsoft Dynamics 365 offers a customizable CRM solution that integrates with other Microsoft products, such as Outlook and Excel. It provides sales teams with tools for lead management, pipeline tracking, and sales forecasting.

Sales Analytics and Reporting Tools:

4. Tableau: Tableau is a leading data visualization and analytics platform that enables sales teams to create interactive dashboards and reports. It allows users to analyze sales data, identify trends, and gain actionable insights to drive informed decision-making.

5. Microsoft Power BI: Microsoft Power BI is a powerful business intelligence tool that enables users to visualize and analyze data from multiple sources. It provides sales teams with tools for creating interactive reports, exploring data, and sharing insights with stakeholders.

6. Google Analytics: Google Analytics is a web analytics platform that provides valuable insights into website traffic, user behavior, and conversion rates. Sales teams can use Google Analytics to track the performance of online sales channels, optimize marketing campaigns, and improve website conversion rates.

Sales Enablement Platforms:

7. Seismic: Seismic is a sales enablement platform that helps organizations deliver personalized content and sales collateral to their sales teams. It provides tools for content management, sales automation, and analytics, enabling sales reps to engage customers more effectively and drive sales.

8. Highspot: Highspot is a sales enablement platform that uses AI-driven insights to help sales teams find and deliver the right content to the right audience at the right time. It offers features such as content management, sales coaching, and analytics to empower sales reps and accelerate deal cycles.

Communication and Collaboration Tools:

9. Slack: Slack is a popular messaging and collaboration platform that enables teams to communicate in real-time via chat channels and direct messages. Sales teams can use Slack to share updates, collaborate on projects, and coordinate activities more efficiently.

10. Microsoft Teams: Microsoft Teams is a unified communication and collaboration platform that integrates with other Microsoft Office 365 tools. It provides sales teams with features such as chat, video conferencing, file sharing, and project management, enabling seamless collaboration across the organization.

Sales Productivity and Automation Tools:

11. Outreach: Outreach is a sales engagement platform that helps sales teams automate and personalize their outreach efforts. It provides tools for email sequencing, prospecting, and analytics, allowing sales reps to engage prospects at scale while maintaining a personalized touch.

12. SalesLoft: SalesLoft is a sales engagement platform that helps sales teams automate repetitive tasks and streamline their sales workflows. It offers features such as email tracking, cadence management, and analytics to drive efficiency and effectiveness in sales prospecting and outreach.

Conclusion:

The software and platforms mentioned above represent just a fraction of the myriad tools available to sales organizations today. By leveraging these technologies effectively, sales teams can enhance their productivity, streamline processes, and drive better outcomes for their businesses. However, it's essential to choose tools that align with your organization's specific needs, goals, and workflows to maximize their impact on sales performance and growth. Additionally, staying informed about emerging trends and innovations in sales technology will be crucial for staying competitive in the rapidly evolving sales landscape.

Conclusion

In the ever-evolving landscape of sales, where competition is fierce and markets fluctuate, understanding and leveraging sales metrics and analytics is paramount for sustained growth and success. Throughout the pages of "Sales Metrics and Analytics: Tracking Performance for Growth," we have delved into the intricacies of this dynamic field, exploring various metrics, tools, and strategies that empower businesses to make informed decisions, optimize performance, and drive profitability.

As we reach the conclusion of this journey, it is essential to reflect on the significance of the insights shared within these pages. Sales metrics and analytics serve as the compass guiding organizations through the complexities of the modern marketplace, providing invaluable insights into customer behavior, sales performance, and market trends. By harnessing the power of data, businesses can uncover hidden opportunities, mitigate risks, and align their strategies with the evolving needs of their target audience.

To our readers, we extend our heartfelt gratitude for embarking on this exploration with us. Your commitment to enhancing your understanding of sales metrics and analytics not only demonstrates your dedication to professional growth but also underscores your commitment to driving excellence within your organization. We recognize the time and effort you have invested in engaging with the material presented in this book, and we sincerely hope that the knowledge gained will serve as a catalyst for transformative change in your sales endeavors.

We would also like to express our appreciation to the countless professionals, researchers, and thought leaders whose contributions have shaped the landscape of sales metrics and analytics. Their pioneering work has paved the way for innovation and continuous improvement in this field, enriching our understanding and expanding the horizons of what is possible.

As we part ways, we encourage you to continue your journey of exploration and discovery. The realm of sales metrics and analytics is vast and ever-evolving, offering limitless opportunities for learning and growth. Whether you are a seasoned veteran or a novice in the *field, there is always something new to discover, a fresh perspective to gain, and a novel approach to explore.*

In closing, let us remember that the true measure of success lies not only in the attainment of goals but also in the journey taken to reach them. May the insights gleaned from this book empower you to chart a course towards greater success, prosperity, and fulfillment in your sales endeavors.

Thank you once again for choosing "Sales Metrics and Analytics: Tracking Performance for Growth" as your guide. May your path be illuminated by the light of knowledge, and may your efforts be rewarded with unparalleled success.

With warm regards

www.ingramcontent.com/pod-product-compliance
Lightning Source LLC
Chambersburg PA
CBHW062101220526
45471CB00010B/3558